BEING A NATION STATE IN THE TWENTY-FIRST CENTURY

Between State and Synagogue in Modern Israel

BEING A NATION STATE IN THE TWENTY-FIRST CENTURY

Between State and Synagogue in Modern Israel

SHUKI FRIEDMAN

Preface by Justice Elyakim Rubinstein

BOSTON
2023

Library of Congress Cataloging-in-Publication Data

Names: Fridman, Shuḳi, author.
Title: Being a nation state in the twenty-first century : between state and synagogue in modern Israel / Shuki Friedman.
Description: Boston : Academic Studies Press, 2023. | Series: Judaism and Jewish life | Includes bibliographical references and index.
Identifiers: LCCN 2022049492 (print) | LCCN 2022049493 (ebook) | ISBN 9798887190891 (hardback) | ISBN 9798887190907 (adobe pdf) | ISBN 9798887190914 (epub)
Subjects: LCSH: Judaism and state--Israel. | Religion and state--Israel. | Jews--Identity.
Classification: LCC BM538.S7 F75 2023 (print) | LCC BM538.S7 (ebook) | DDC 296.095694--dc23/eng/20221027
LC record available at https://lccn.loc.gov/2022049492
LC ebook record available at https://lccn.loc.gov/2022049493

ISBN 9798887190891 (hardback)
ISBN 9798887190907 (adobe pdf)
ISBN 9798887190914 (epub)

Cover design by Ivan Grave
Book design by Lapiz Digital Services

Published by Academic Studies Press.
1577 Beacon Street
Brookline, MA 02446, USA
press@academicstudiespress.com
www.academicstudiespress.com

Contents

My Journey for Change: Personal Introduction and Acknowledgments

Over the last twenty years I have worked to promote new arrangements with respect to the main issues that characterize the relationship between religion and state in Israel. In the meeting rooms of government ministries, in the discussion rooms of Knesset committees, in my public activity and in any other way that I believed could lead the State of Israel to the desired goal: strengthening its Jewish and democratic identity and calming the severe social tensions that are tearing Israeli society apart as a result of disagreements around the proper balance between religion and the state, or if you wish, between "church and state" in Israel.

As someone who works both to promote political and social change, as well as in the field of academic and applied research, my public advocacy has gone hand in hand with an array of research endeavors to better understand the terrain in which I operate. I have extensively studied the moral, legal, and historical components of religion-state relations in Israel, which together constitute the "status quo" that has framed—rather uneasily—these relations for many years.

This book is the fruit of my studies, but it also reveals the insights of someone who has worked to effect real change, not just to write about it from a safe academic distance.

I would like to take this opportunity to thank my friends and colleagues in the research field and in the "real world" for sharing this goal through their true cooperation; our stimulating, sometimes challenging, conversations and their wise insights are reflected in this book. My thanks go to former Knesset member and renowned attorney Nachum Langental, with whom I began this practical and intellectual journey as a young law student; to my teacher and partner of many years, Professor Yedidia Stern; to my colleagues at the Peres Academic Center, the Israel Democracy Institute, and the Jewish People Policy Institute (JPPI); and to the many others who have been my intellectual partners and fellow seekers along the road toward change.

The book before you is based on a study of the religion-state "status-quo" I published with the Israel Democracy Institute. I thank the IDI for being my professional home during that period and for its unfailing support in publishing that research. This book is published with the assistance of my two current professional homes, the Jewish People Policy Institute (JPPI), and the Peres Academic Center. They have my gratitude.

Last but not least, I would like to thank my wife Oshrit and our children, who accompany and support me wherever I am. I am beyond grateful for that.

—Shuki Friedman

Preface

On State and Religion in Israel

Judaism is a unique entity. It is a religion and a culture, but also a national entity. The State of Israel, the fulfillment of a dream of two millennia, when without a foothold in the promised land, Jewish continued existence depended on religious, spiritual, and intellectual values. But how can this state, Jewish and democratic, relate to state and religion matters?

It is a complex issue. The Jewish population in Israel—about 80%—is not of a unified character: there are secular, traditional, orthodox, and ultraorthodox Jews, as well as small conservative and reform congregations. The spectrum is wide, and so are the issues: conversion, marriage and divorce, Kashrut, Shabbat—each of those is subject to major controversies, many of which are dividing society. I am writing having served in a number of public offices—Government Secretary under Prime Ministers Shamir and Rabin, Attorney General and Justice of the Supreme Court, and peace negotiator—and having been involved in decisions on each of these subjects.

Shuki Friedman, in his concise but very informative, balanced, and well-organized book, surveys the issues systematically and describes the development of state and religion issues since the establishment of Israel. A main motive is the erosion of what used to be the «Status Quo» agreed upon and implemented by 1948, which tried to «freeze» the pre-state situation in this regard. In the principal areas of contention—conversion to Judaism, marriage and divorce,

Shabbat and Kashrut—great changes have occurred over the years in Israeli social life and strata, which have changed the landscape and eroded the historic foundations.

I can personally attest to the changes and the efforts to find harmonious solutions to these issues. As Government Secretary, Attorney General and Justice (as well as Deputy Chief of Mission in our Washington Embassy), I was involved in negotiations and litigation concerning conversion in particular. My view has always been that we should look for harmony among the various Jewish trends. Sadly, it did not succeed. Contentions exist also in the other aforementioned areas. No government and Knesset succeeded in carving relevant legislation, and it fell to the Supreme Court to decide—which makes the Court controversial in certain circles of Israeli society and body politic.

Our author concludes by advocating a regulatory change, dividing the subjects between those that should be regulated, such as conversion and marriage and divorce, and those that should be left to private initiatives, such as Kashrut. Shabbat is of a third category, the public face of Israel on the day of rest, with other complexities.

Dr. Friedman should be commended for a meticulous and analytical achievement, highly readable. While it is difficult, given the political constraints, to be optimistic about agreed solutions, this work serves as very useful guide, and provides a glimpse of hope.

Justice Elyakim Rubinstein

Introduction: "A People that Lives Apart"—the Uniqueness of Israel between Nation States

"I see a people that lives apart," said the prophet Balaam about the people of Israel (Numbers 23:9) and indeed, at least from the perspective of church and state relations in Israel, Balaam was right. The State of Israel is unique, different from any other country in the world. This book deals with the interplay between religion and state in Israel and seeks to provide a perspective on and meaning to these relations. But to allow a better understanding of the conflicts over the Jewish identity of the State of Israel, described throughout the book, I will begin with a broad overview of Israel's identity axes, the constitutional regime built along with them, and the rifts that characterize Israeli society.

Israel is a nation-state. It is the nation-state of the Jewish people. But unlike other nation-states, the fundamental defining feature of the Jewish nation-state is its Jewishness. The State of Israel, as determined constitutionally, is a Jewish (and democratic) state. It is the world's only Jewish state. One might ask: Other nation-states are also unique, what makes Israel special? Whereas in other nation-states, several characteristics, apart from territory, bind the citizens of the state and make them the people, the fundamental and central definition of the State of Israel is its Jewishness—an identity component that results from interweaving almost inextricable ethnic and religious affiliation. Therefore, while in other nation-states an immigrant or a minority member can usually choose to feel at home within the national identity, even if not perfectly, a non-Jew will never fully be a national member of the Jewish nation-state.

For those who grew up with the American constitutional tradition, which regards the First Amendment's Non-establishment clause as a core element of its national foundational framework, it is difficult to understand how different the State of Israel is in this respect. In contrast to the American wall of separation between church and state, in Israel the Jewish religion is deeply rooted and integrated into the country's constitutional mechanisms of government. This is easily illustrated by its allocation of a budget to religious issues. In the US, issues such as funding transportation to religious schools or using public school facilities after school for religious purposes have long been the subject of sharp debate. In fact, the US Supreme Court is currently debating its long tradition of rulings limiting the scope of legitimate public funding of religious education.[1] In contrast, in Israel, religious studies are the core curriculum of about 40% of the schools in the formal, state-financed education system. The scope of the funding allocated for this, and for other distinctly Jewish-religious purposes, is enormous and constitutes a significant percentage of the of the State of Israel's budget.

Even for the European observer familiar with the tradition of the Christian state, understanding the situation in Israel is not intuitive. While a fundamental precept of Christianity calls for the separation of the kingdom of heaven from the kingdom of man, Judaism in its fundamentalist form advocates an all-encompassing rule of heaven, including the management of the affairs of the kingdom of man—the state. In this respect, Judaism is somewhat similar to its sister religion, Islam. As in Judaism, in Islam the word of God as expressed in Sharia, Muslim law, should regulate the conduct of state affairs. But even with regard to Islam and the Muslim countries, Israel is special. In some Muslim countries, Islamic identity is indeed a cornerstone of government and constitutionality, but it is not the single defining feature of their unique national distinctiveness. After all, there are dozens of Muslim nation-states in the world, which, despite their common religious denominator, differ from one another, and in too many cases also fight each other.

---

1 On the First Amendment in the US Supreme Court see: Benjamin Justice, "The Originalist Case Against Vouchers: The First Ammendment, Religion, and American Public Education," American Public Education (October 1, 2014), https://papers.ssrn.com/sol3/papers.cfm?abstract_id=2494890; Klint Alexander, "The Road to Vouchers: The Supreme Court's Compliance and the Crumbling of the Wall between the Separation of Church and Stat in American Education," Kentucky Law Journal 92, no. 2 (2003), https://uknowledge.uky.edu/cgi/viewcontent.cgi?article=1401&context=klj.

What, then, makes Judaism such a unique defining element of a nation-state and one that makes the state of Israel a unique case among nation-states? To understand this, one can turn to Jewish history. In a nutshell, Jewish history ranges from a sovereign or semi-sovereign existence for about a thousand years in the Land of Israel, two thousand years ago, to a decentralized existence of two thousand years in the Diaspora. This history has created an identity compound that mixes classic national elements of territory, language, and common past, with identity definitions that stem from the Jewish religion and rely on Jewish law as created mainly after the period of Jewish national sovereignty. This Halachah built legal walls around the Jews, in order to preserve a religious but also ethnic identity uniqueness and thus preserve, despite the geographical dispersion, the Jewish nation. This strategy, it should be noted, has been a phenomenal success.

Among scholars of the phenomenon of nationalism, there is well-known controversy as to the "nationalism" of the Jewish people that well illustrates the unique identity complexity of Judaism. On the one hand, some scholars of nationalism, those of the modernian school, including Eric Hobsbawm and Benedict Anderson, argue that Judaism is a religion and therefore Jewish nationalism is fundamentally an ontological impossibility. On the other hand, scholars of nationalism belonging to the ethno-symbolic school, including Anthony Smith, believe that the Jewish people is the model of an ancient nationalism that has been renewed.

At the turn of the nineteenth century, carried on the waves of the European "Springtime of Nations," the founding fathers of the State of Israel sought to establish a Jewish nation-state in the Land of Israel. From the first Zionist Congress in 1897 to the present day, the definitional challenge of Judaism and its definition disturbs, and perhaps even haunts, the Jewish state. What is the Jewishness of the Jewish state? The first Zionists asked themselves this question and it is still being asked by the citizens of twenty-first-century Israel. Is it the secular-national expression of what Judaism was until Zionism and the establishment of the state and its religious components a shell that should be shed? Is it the traditional commitment to the legal-halachic norms and rules of Judaism as shaped in the Oral Torah that should be its identity compass? Or is there some balance to be struck between these two ideas?

The issue that most clearly illustrates the entanglement of Jewish identity and the relationship between the State of Israel and its Judaism (and which I will address in more detail below) is the question of "who is a Jew" or what defines Jewishness in the eyes of the state. It can be assumed that in the very distant past, at the beginning of Jewish sovereignty, well before exile, the basis for belonging to the Jewish people was purely tribal-ethnic, and joining this people, as the book of Ruth teaches us, was simply a matter of will. Over the years, in the Diaspora, alongside the ghetto walls, the walls of Jewish identity also rose. Joining and belonging to what was predominantly an innate Judaism was conditional on the conversion process which requires a complete willingness to keep the commandments of the Jewish law—the Halacha. During these long years of life in the Diaspora, the clear defining element of Judaism was religion, and it was Jewish law that determined who could enter its gates. With the advent of Zionism, and even more so with the establishment of the Jewish state, the question of the definition of Judaism became much sharper. This is because the essential, central defining element of the Jewish state is that the majority of its citizens are Jews.

By virtue of the Law of Return, which states that every Jew can immigrate to Israel, Judaism is key to Israeli citizenship. But what is it? Ben-Gurion, the founding father of the Jewish state, wanted to establish a secular Jewish state in the Land of Israel. He wanted the young nation-state to set the boundaries of Judaism and its definitions. In matters concerning the society established in the Land of Israel, such as its entrance gate and its recognition of one's Jewishness formulated national-secular definitions that were not bound by the religious-halachic standard. To his distress, a political crisis surrounding the definition of Judaism erupted, and when he saw that he might lose to the religious politicians, Ben-Gurion turned to the "sages of Israel." He wrote to a number of Jewish thinkers, many of them not religious, and asked them what they thought defined Judaism. The "sages of Israel" disappointed Ben-Gurion. Although they presented a wide variety of possibilities for Jewish identity as a matter of principle, most of them admitted that there is a religious component to Jewish identity that is not easily neutralized. They thought this was true even in the case of Jewish nationalism, and that it was expressed in the secular Jewish state, which had opened a new definitional space.

Israel has no written constitution. The never-ending debate about the meaning of its Jewish identity when founded is one of the reasons for this. But over the years, the State of Israel has created a constitution that is based on its Declaration of Independence and made up of the Basic Laws that have been enacted, one by one, throughout the seventy-four years of the state's existence. Both the Declaration of Independence and the Basic Laws enacted in 1992 enshrined the dual, complicated nature of Israel as a "Jewish and democratic state." In so doing, the constitution of the state rests on a foundation with significant potential for conflict. Democracy in the thick sense—substantial/liberal democracy—means the uncompromising adoption of a long line of liberal values and human rights. Judaism in the full and fundamental sense implies obedience to Jewish laws and norms, some of which are in contradiction with liberal values. In addition, Jewish nationalism in the broader and more extreme sense means, at least in the eyes of some Israelis, reduced rights for the Arab minority.

This debate is significantly reflected in the daily political, sociocultural existence of the State of Israel. Two major schisms have divided Israeli society since its inception: the Jewish-Arab rift, and the religious-secular rift. At the heart of the Arab-Jewish rift is a dispute over the balance between the Jewishness—in the national sense—of the state and the rights of the large Arab minority living in it. At the heart of the religious-secular rift is controversy over the significance of the state's Jewish nature, in the religious sense, and the expression that should be given to the state's Jewishness in general, especially when it conflicts with other rights and values. These rifts have many legal, structural, and practical expressions.

There are many interconnections between these rifts. The debate over Judaism—in the religious sense of the state—impacts the debate around Judaism in the national sense, and vice versa. Therefore, the two rifts described have mutual implications and consequences. And yet in everyday Israeli reality most of the controversial issues that are at the seam between the components of Israel's identity can be associated with one of these rifts. This can be illustrated as a tension moving along two axes: one between Judaism, in the national sense, and democracy; the other between Judaism, in the religious sense, and democracy. The subject of this book is the internal Jewish rift and the debate that is animated by a triangle of relations between democratic-liberal Israel, Jewish-national Israel, and Jewish-religious Israel. Some issues carry both tensions, others only one.

Israel is seventy-four years old, but the debate over the character of the state began in the early days of the Zionist movement. At first, when Zionism was simply an idea, the debate was purely ideological. To the extent that the idea found practical expression in the initiation of Jewish settlement in the Land of Israel, this debate also took on concrete aspects in the daily reality of the Zionist enterprise. Dilemmas regarding Sabbath observance versus individual liberties, shared public education versus the segregation of religious and nonreligious schools, the management of religious services, and more, were already prominent for the pioneers of the renewed Jewish settlement in the Land of Israel.

These debates, which have become a constant struggle between people with different worldviews in all arenas of the State of Israel, are the subject of this book. Each of the concrete issues it deals with, those framed as part of the Status Quo in religious-state relations, are expressions of the root and principled debate about the nature of Israeli-religious Judaism and the proper balance between it and the Jewish-national and democratic-liberal components. Therefore, the story of the Status Quo and the way in which it has been shaped, eroded, and updated since the founding of Israel until today should be read from this broad perspective. The debate is not about the least number of bus lines that should operate on Shabbat, but about the balance between freedom of movement and relinquishing it in deference to Jewish law, which prohibits traveling on Shabbat. The debate is not about how kashrut services will be delivered, but about the monopoly of the rabbinical establishment, if you will, over the state's affairs in the religious sphere and more generally, and so on.

The bitter debate over the character of the State of Israel has a significant impact on its nature as a liberal and open state and its place among Western liberal-democratic states. This debate also has significant direct and indirect effects on Jews living outside Israel. Many of these Jews see Israel as their second home. Some of the arrangements discussed in this book, including the issue of the definition of Judaism ("who is a Jew"), directly affect the way Jews outside Israel view their Jewish identity, as the Jewish state's decisions with regard to various matters have an impact on them. Other issues affect the image of Israel in the eyes of some of these Jews, most of whom, in the United States and other countries, are secular and liberal. These Jews find it increasingly difficult to admire and connect with the State of Israel as long as it chooses a more pronounced and conservative Jewish-religious-national identity, with practical expressions in the Israeli reality.

The book is structured as a broad framework story that describes the history of the relationship between religion and state in Israel while addressing each of the concrete issues that constitute this relationship. It describes the cornerstones that established the relationship, the factors that led to changes in the various arrangements and in the broader picture and in reality as it is today. It is my hope that anyone who has an interest in understanding the contemporary State of Israel and its challenges will find it useful and illuminating.

1

Jewish and Democratic—On Church-State Relations in Israel

The classic term "Status Quo"[1] has been used for more than seven decades to describe the relationship between religion and state in Israel;[2] the history of the term is also the history of this relationship. It includes a complex network of de jure and de facto arrangements that govern areas where the Jewish religion and the State of Israel coincide, generate friction, or come into conflict. The use of "Status Quo" in this sense has become so self-evident that many coalition agreements over the years[3] have employed the term to describe the relationship between religion and state before the signing of the agreement and to anchor

---

1 "Status quo ante bellum" is a Latin phrase whose meaning is "the situation before the war." This, in the shortened forms "Status Quo ante" and "Status Quo" has come to mean the existing state of affairs at a particular time in the past or present.

2 The relationship between religion and state in Israel—that is, between the Jewish religion and the State of Israel—has two main dimensions, the national and the religious. The former refers to the interplay between Israel as the nation-state of the Jewish people and as a democratic state (the Jewish-Arab divide). The latter involves the limits of the Jewishness of the state and the legal and practical arrangements that regulate the relations between religion and state and translate them into public and official conduct. In this book I refer mainly to the second dimension, and specifically to these arrangements and their impact on the character of the state as a Jewish state. See Ruth Gavison, "A Jewish and Democratic State: Political Identity, Ideology and Law," *Tel Aviv University Law Review* 19, no. 3 (1995): 631–82 [Heb.].

3 See, for example, David Ben-Gurion's commitment to the religious parties, in 1955, that his new government's basic guidelines would specify adherence to the Status Quo and that

the new government's commitment to preserve the existing situation insofar as government action is concerned.[4]

On many issues there is a convergence of religion and state. The most important of these are Sabbath observance in the public sphere; marriage and divorce; parallel school systems; conversion to Judaism; kashrut (Jewish dietary laws); and the provision of religious services. Other issues that fall under this rubric are burial, the military conscription of yeshiva students, the inclusion of religious content in school curricula, the exclusion of women in the public sphere, religious observance in the armed forces, organ donations, euthanasia, autopsies, holy sites, hametz (leavened products) on Passover, pig farming, and the import of nonkosher meat. In this study, I have focused on the main issues that are traditionally included in the Status Quo—the Sabbath, marriage and divorce, conversion, and kashrut—because of their impact on life in Israel and on Israel-Diaspora relations, but also because most of them were included in the Status Quo when it gelled before the establishment of the state and can accordingly be used to demonstrate its erosion over the years.[5]

---

they would advance no new demands related to religious observances. See M. Shmaryahu, "Finishing Up the Draft of the Coalition Guidelines," *Maariv*, Sept. 15, 1955 [Heb.]. The coalition agreement between United Torah Judaism and the Likud, in advance of the formation of the thirty-fourth government in 2015, provided that "the Status Quo on issues of religion and state in Israel will be preserved as it has been for decades." See http://main.knesset.gov.il/mk/government/documents/Coalition2015_2.pdf, 6. See also: the 2009 coalition agreement between Shas and the Likud prior to the formation of the thirty-second government (http://main.knesset.gov.il/mk/government/documents/coal2009Shas.pdf); the agreement between Shas and Kadima before the establishment of the thirty-first government in 2006 (http://main.knesset.gov.il/mk/government/documents/Coal2006shas.pdf); the agreement between the Likud and United Torah Judaism prior to the formation of the twenty-ninth government in 2001 (http://main.knesset.gov.il/mk/government/documents/coal2001yht.pdf).

4 Another instructive example is the coalition agreement signed by the Labor Party and Shas before the establishment of the twenty-fifth government in 1992, whereby "if the Status Quo in religious matters is violated, the parties undertake to amend the violation by appropriate legislation." The next section of that agreement specifies that "the Prime Minister will appoint a five-member committee of jurists who will recommend, within a hundred days of the date of this agreement, appropriate legislation to anchor the Status Quo in matters of religion and ensure its existence and preservation" (http://main.knesset.gov.il/mk/government/Pages/CoalitionAgreements.aspx). A majority opinion of the High Court of Justice refused to invalidate the agreement, on the grounds that the court recognizes the Knesset's authority to legislate matters of religion and state, even when the court has spoken and ruled otherwise. In an aside, Justice Aharon Barak (then the vice president of the court) recognized the existence of the Status Quo in matters of religion and state and its legitimacy. See HCJ 5364/94, Vilner v. the Chair of the Israel Labor Party, PD 49 (1) 758, 784 (1995).

5 See below. Surprisingly, there is no full mapping of the issues of religion and state in Israel, despite the quantity of writing in the field. I am not excused from the matter.

The Status Quo comprises both a symbolic dimension[6] and concrete arrangements.[7] On the symbolic level, it is the Archimedean point of the relations between religion and state, a "living creature in its environment" that is constantly changing.[8] On the regulatory level, it is the result of normative compliance, ad hoc arrangements, national and local political compromises, court rulings, and a reality that often reflects the erosion of all of these.

The arrangements that created and shaped the initial Status Quo were forged at the establishment of the state and in the early years of independence. Since then, these arrangements have undergone constant modification and erosion for several reasons: changes in Israeli society and its values, changes in the composition of the Israeli population, judicial activism, efforts by civil society organizations to promote religious pluralism, and the nonreligious population's growing awareness of the nature of the religious services they wish to enjoy or are forced to consume.

All these factors are eating away at the Status Quo and affect the Jewish character of the state as expressed in concrete arrangements. This trend further sharpens the question of what is "Jewish" in the Jewish state. They also lead to a confused situation. On the one hand, the courts and the real world continue to chip away at the existing arrangements, leaving islands of regulated issues in a sea of nonobservance, or incoherent regulations; on the other hand, the legislature and the political system find themselves with no real ability to reach an accord on these matters.[9]

The trend is not uniform and is not always significant. For example, there are those who allege that the growing presence of religion in the education system (a component of "the Status Quo Letter"),[10] for which they have coined

---

6 Or an "unwritten social charter," as Aviezer Ravitzky called it in *Religious and Secular in Israel: A Kulturkampf?* (Jerusalem: The Israel Democracy Institute, 1997), 15.

7 This study focuses on the practical arrangements rather than on the fundamental philosophical questions about the very legitimacy of these arrangements in the liberal sense. For a philosophical perspective on the appropriate and justifiable relationship, see Gideon Sapir and Danny Statman, *State and Religion in Israel: A Philosophical-Legal Inquiry* (Cambridge: Cambridge University Press, 2019), 9–40

8 Thus Justice Yoel Sussman, in HCJ 58/68, Shalit v. Minister of the Interior, PD 23 (2) 477, 513 (1970).

9 Guy Ben-Porat has dealt with several aspects of the relationship between religion and state in Israel in several respects. He focuses on the public sphere and what I call the "change from below" in that relationship. Ben-Porat shows how several factors, including market forces, ideology, the courts, and the lack of governance have led to the secularization of public space. See Guy Ben-Porat, *Between State and Synagogue: The Secularization of Contemporary Israel* (Cambridge: Cambridge University Press, 2013), 1–26.

10 See below, note 11.

the neologism "religionization," aims to equate Judaism with its Orthodox interpretation and to implement unequal budgeting of the secular and religious school systems.[11] This, they say, undermines the Status Quo by opening the secular system to increased religious influence.[12] Because this issue does not fall squarely into the normal acceptation of religion-and-state legislative state arrangements and does not have a strong normative expression, I will not consider it further in this study.[13]

---

11 According to the Secular Forum, an organization at the forefront of the campaign against religionization in Israel, religious discourse has penetrated the public education system from various directions, with the encouragement of the Ministry of Education, which is now dominated by religious and nationalist elements (The Secular Forum website: https://www.hiloni.org.il/hadata-handle/what-is-hadata). The forum, as well as a number of journalists and public figures (e.g., Or Kashti, "[Education Minister] Bennett Says There Is No Religionization; The Money, the Books, and the Curriculum He Is so Proud of Prove Otherwise," *Ha'aretz*, July 7, 2007 [Heb.], https://www.haaretz.co.il/news/education/.premium-1.4235956), the secular education system is liable to change its character as a result of this push. A study published by Molad, a progressive research institute, "Winning Souls: How the Religious Right Has Taken Over Values Education in the Secular Schools" (Molad website, Center for the Renewal of Democracy: http://www.molad.org/images/upload/files/ZehutMasa.pdf), concludes, in brief that, funded by government budgets and with political support, religious organizations are penetrating the secular school system and disseminating their religious-conservative-right wing notion of Jewish identity. By contrast, the Knesset Research and Information Center investigated the issue and found that these claims are not borne out. See "Information on the Involvement of External Elements in Educational Activities in the Schools" (Knesset website: https://www.knesset.gov.il/mmm/data/pdf/m04025.pdf) [Heb.].

The Status Quo Letter (See S. Ilan Troen and Noah Lucas, eds., *Israel: The First Decade of Independence* [Albany: SUNY Press, 1995], 78–79) states that the "full autonomy of every educational stream will be assured." It can be inferred that this paragraph might mean that forcing religious content into the secular school system is a departure from the Status Quo. It can be countered, of course, that even if this is the case and there is indeed an attempt to inject more religious content into the secular system, this does not violate the Status Quo, which merely ensures the independence of the different streams of education. Moreover, the alleged religionization of education is a phenomenon only of the last two or three years, and hence cannot be seen as an ongoing erosion of the Status Quo.

12 Shuki Friedman, "The 'Religionization' of Israel Is Troubling, but the Fears about It Are Hysterical," jta.org, June 28, 2016, https://www.jta.org/2016/06/28/opinion/the-religionization-of-israel-is-troubling-but-the-fears-about-it-are-hysterical.

13 Another alleged arena of is religionization is the IDF. Although there has never been a clear Status Quo in the military, some believe that there are increasing manifestations of religious influence there. See Yagil Levy, "The Theocratization of the Israeli Military," *Armed Forces & Society* 40 (2013), 269–294. See also: Yagil Levy, *The Divine Commander in Chief: The Theocratization of the Israeli Military* (Tel Aviv: Am Oved, 2015), 9 [Heb.]. Others hold that the IDF is becoming more secular, as shown by the integration of women into many positions and units and the adoption of liberal values by within the military education system. A vehement spokesman of this school is Rabbi Yigal Lowenstein, the cofounder of the Bnei David premilitary academy in Eli. See: Shimon Cohen, "Rabbi Lowenstein in a Letter to the Graduates of Bnei David," *Arutz* 7, March 27, 2017, https://www.inn.co.il/News/News.aspx/343098.

One thing has not changed, however. For seventy-two years, issues of religion and state have been at the heart of an ongoing political and public controversy.[14] As a result of the political power relations just before and after independence, and today as well, these issues have repeatedly triggered coalition crises that sometimes threaten and actually do bring down the government.[15] The relative strength of the religious and secular has not changed dramatically over the years; today, too, the religious parties can tip the balance and determine which secular party heads the coalition.[16] The struggle between the sectors over the character of the Israeli public sphere, with regard to religion and state, has continued along much the same lines from the early days of the state to the present.

On the other hand, out of an understanding of the importance of easing the tensions between the different sectors of Israeli society, attempts have been made to arrive at new arrangements, through compacts proposed by civil society elements,[17] as well as through action by the political echelons.[18] Although the compact documents received broad popular support, the political expression of their proposals has been limited. Many of them were formulated into bills and submitted to the Knesset, but the traditional veto exercised by the religious and ultraorthodox parties and the opposition of rabbis from all across the Orthodox spectrum to any compromise on issues of religion and state has meant that none of them became law. Hence the impasse persists and no new arrangements have been established.

---

14 That was highlighted in the second general election campaign in 2019, in which state-and-religion relations were a main topic of the public debate.

15 At the end of 2017, Minister of Health Yaakov Litzman of the ultraorthodox United Torah Judaism party resigned his portfolio after the government permitted Israel Railways to perform infrastructure work on the Sabbath. The Shas party has threatened to quit the coalition if the Municipalities Ordinance is not amended so as to restrict the interior minister's authority to approve local bylaws that permit commercial activity on the Sabbath. See: Tal Shalev and Yaki Adamker, "Litzman Resigns from Government Following the Railroad Crisis: 'They Have Violated the Status Quo,'" *Walla!*, November 26, 2007, https://news.walla.co.il/item/3114380; Haim Levinson, "Deri Threatens: If the Supermarkets Law Doesn't Pass Tonight, I Will Resign," *Ha'aretz*, December 11, 2017, https://www.haaretz.co.il/news/politi/1.4678197. See also Itzhak Galnoor and Dana Blander, *The Political System of Israel*, 2 vols. (Tel Aviv: Am Oved, and Jerusalem: Israel Democracy Institute, 2013), 1027 [Heb.].

16 For a discussion of the significance and power of the satellite parties, including the ultraorthodox, see *Recommendations for Reform of the System of Government and Action Plan* (Jerusalem: The Israel Democracy Institute, 2011), 36–37; Shlomo Hasson, *State and Religion in Israel: Possible Scenarios* (College Park: Gildenhorn Institute for Israel Studies at the University of Maryland, 2015), 43.

17 See below, p. 86.

18 See below, p. 78.

The chapters that follow focus on a description of the current relations between religion and state, rather than on some ideal situation. They show that the Status Quo is a hollow shell that should be replaced by coherent arrangements that govern issues of religion and state in Israel. I also examine whether there is any point in trying to regulate these relations by means of legislation—as tested by the possibility of enforcing it—and whether informal attempts at regulation have any prospect of success. In conclusion, I will argue that it is appropriate to preserve only an essential core of arrangements that derive from religion-state relations, while expressing the country's Jewish identity in other ways. There is a place for a minimum of arrangements aimed at preserving a Jewish framework for the State of Israel, while working to strengthen its Jewish identity in ways that express its Jewishness on the ethical, cultural, and educational planes.

2

The Shaping of the Status Quo

The Basic Elements of the Status Quo in Matters of Religion and State

The Status Quo in matters of religion and state is an "imagined reality"[1]—and that fluidity works to its advantage. Each side can see in it whatever it desires.[2] As a result, over the years the Status Quo has acquired the status of a magic spell, used by politicians[3] and even the courts to denote the relationship between religion and state.[4]

---

1 Benedict Anderson coined the term "imagined communities" to describe the phenomenon of nationalism as a reality created by the imagination of members of the community. In our context, the Status Quo is an imagined reality in the sense that the term is believed to express a concrete reality, when in fact the situation is fluid and depends on a perspective and a point in time.

2 See Daphna Barak-Erez, "Law and Religion under the Status Quo Model: Between Past Compromises and Constant Change," *Cardozo Law Review* 30, no. 6): 2495.

3 See, e.g., "Status Quo in Matters of Religion and State Will Be Preserved," *Ha'aretz*, March 7, 2001, and the aforementioned coalition agreements.

4 See: HCJ 5016/96, Horev v. Minister of Transport, P. D. 51 (4)1 (1997); HCJ 5364/94, Vilner v. Prime Minister, P. D. 49(1) 758 (1995); HCJ 5073/91, Israel Theaters Ltd. v. The Municipality of Netanya, P. D. 47(3) 192 (1993); HCJ 3872/93, Meatrael Ltd. v. Prime Minister and Minister of Religious Affairs P. D. 50 (5) (15) 1996.

The term and its initial formulation derive from two main sources: (1) a letter that David Ben-Gurion wrote to the leaders of the ultraorthodox Agudat Israel party in 1947;[5] (2) the various arrangements that prevailed in such matters in Mandatory Palestine. These were reflected in memoranda composed by Zerach Warhaftig, the director of the Law and Justice Department of the Va'ad Leumi ("National Committee"—the prestate shadow government of the Yishuv or Jewish community). Warhaftig used this expression to describe the relationship between religion and state.[6] Some of its elements were common practice and informal agreements.[7]

I will now present the "Status Quo Letter" and the Status Quo arrangements that Warhaftig pointed out.[8]

The Status Quo Letter

Historical Background

In 1947, after the British announced their intention to withdraw as the Mandatory power in Palestine, the United Nations established the Special Committee on Palestine (UNSCOP) to submit recommendations for the future of the territory. Two options were considered: a unitary state, which would necessarily have an Arab majority, or partition, which would give the Jews sovereignty over a reduced territory. The Arabs rejected partition out of hand. The Yishuv leadership and the

---

5 Chronologically, the Status Quo Letter antedated Warhaftig's memoranda and coinage of the term "Status Quo" in this context. Its first application to Ben-Gurion's letter appeared in Moshe Prager, "This Is the History of the Status Quo," *Beit Ya'akov* 62–63 (5724 [1963/4]): 18 [Heb.]. Warhaftig explained his choice of the term in his book on religion and state. See: Zerach Warhaftig, *Constitution of Israel, Religion and State* (Jerusalem: Mesillot, 1988), 64 [Heb.]. (Warhaftig: Constitution) This was noted by Yoel Rappel, "Where Is the Status Quo?" in Sara and Meir Aharoni, eds., *Personalities and Practices in Israel: Jubilee Book* (Kfar Sava: Miksam, 1998), 127 [Heb.]. See Amichai Radzyner, "Forgotten Foundations of the Law and Administration Ordinance and the Hidden Struggle for Religious and State Arrangements," *Cathedra* 136 (2010): 121n5 [Heb.].

6 See Warhaftig, *Constitution*, 64.

7 The friction between religion and state preceded the establishment of the state by many years and accompanied the Zionist movement from its earliest days. It was one of the stumbling blocks that thwarted the attempts to produce a constitution. See Shuki Friedman and Amichai Radzyner, *The Religious Community and the Constitution: What Can History Teach Us?* Policy Paper 69 (Jerusalem: The Israel Democracy Institute, 2006) [Heb.].

8 Haim Cohen linked the religious and state arrangements covered by the Status Quo Letter with the existing situation at the time, even though the provisions are not identical. See Haim Cohen, "Religious Coercion in Israel," in *Sefer Berenson* vol. 2, ed. Aharon Barak and Haim Berenson (Jerusalem: Nevo, 2000), 297, 305.

Zionist movement supported the idea and invested great effort to win over all factions and communities so as to present a single voice to the committee and the international arena. The ultraorthodox Agudat Israel party was wavering; many within it wanted to oppose the establishment of a Jewish state, on the grounds that a state established and run by secular Jews who did not accept and comply with Jewish religious law would be a curse and not a blessing.[9]

In this situation, Agudat Israel needed to anchor the status of halakhah (Jewish religious law) and key religious precepts in the body of the state in the making. The heads of the Yishuv, led by Ben-Gurion, wanted to reach an agreement with Agudat Israel on this matter in order to gain its support for partition. Aware of the vacillation among the ultraorthodox, they feared that were Agudat Israel to oppose the idea, and in the worst case come out publicly against it, it would put paid to the hope that UNSCOP would recommend partition and the establishment of a Jewish state.[10]

The Content of the Status Quo Letter

The negotiations between Agudat Israel and the Yishuv leaders produced the "Status Quo Letter." There is some uncertainty about the exact circumstances of the composition and transmission of the document, which bore the signatures of David Ben-Gurion, the chairman of the Jewish Agency, and two members of its executive, Rabbi Yehuda Leib Fishman (Maimon)[11] and Yitzhak Gruenbaum.[12] According to Menachem Friedman, an ultraorthodox man named Moshe Prager claimed that he pulled strings behind the scenes; others hold that the letter was delivered to the Agudat Israel Executive Committee following negotiations with Ben-Gurion on the Jewish nature of future Jewish state.[13] But the main question for us is what Ben-Gurion intended to convey in the letter. Can it be seen as the

9 Dan Horowitz and Moshe Lissak, *Origins of the Israeli Polity: Palestine under the Mandate* (Chicago: University of Chicago Press, 1978), 53.

10 Menachem Friedman, "The History of the Status Quo: Religion and State in Israel," in *The Transition from Yishuv to State, 1947–1949: Continuity and Change*, ed. Varda Pilowski (Haifa: University of Haifa and the Herzl Institute for the Study of Zionism, 1990), 47, 55–64.

11 Rabbi Yehuda Leib Fishman Maimon (1875–1962) was one of the founders of the Mizrachi religious Zionist movement. He served on the Jewish Agency Executive and subsequently as a cabinet minister until late 1951.

12 Yitzhak Gruenbaum (1879–1970) was then a member of the Jewish Agency Executive and later served as interior minister in the provisional government.

13 Friedman, "The History of the Status Quo," 48–54 describes the long negotiations that preceded the signing of the letter. Friedman's analysis shows that the agreements were quite basic and not at all a significant achievement, as was later represented by ultraorthodox parties.

first statement of an agreement to maintain a balance of religion and state in the country to be created? Did it constitute a commitment to the Orthodox by the Yishuv establishment regarding the nature of the future relations between religion and state?

The letter has two parts.[14] The first presents the background for its composition and notes that the Jewish Agency Executive cannot make commitments about the constitution of a state that has not yet been established. It is possible that these reservations were included out of caution and the authors' desire to set the record straight and make Agudat Israel aware of the constraints to which they are subject; but it is also possible that this paragraph reflects a limited willingness to implement its promises.

The second part deals with the four issues that were of special concern to Agudat Israel with respect to the place of the Jewish religion in the new state: the Sabbath, kashrut, marriage, and education. The letter is rather vague on the two more problematic issues, Sabbath and marriage. With regard to the former, it promises only that Saturday will be the legal day of rest in the Jewish state. Nothing can be inferred from this, even in general, about the character of the day of rest or about what might be covered by any law regulating the matter. It can even be argued that the phrase "day of rest" hints at a social right and not a religious observance.[15] With regard to marital law, the letter notes that "all member of the Jewish Agency executive recognize the serious nature of the problem and the great difficulties involved" (if the prescriptions of religious law were not followed) and expresses the commitment of all parties "to do all that can be done to satisfy the needs of the religiously observant in this matter and to prevent a rift in the Jewish People." Given the legal situation that prevailed under the Mandate, [16] the authors of the letter could have promised more concrete arrangements, but they merely outlined in vague terms the purpose of the arrangement that would be formulated. In the matter of kashrut, too, the executive promised to ensure the availability of kosher food in state institutions,

---

What is more, even after independence the ultraorthodox did not consider the letter to be an anchor of religion-state arrangements.

14 For the full text, see "Text of the Status Quo Letter," *Israel: The First Decade of Independence*, ed. S. Ilan Troen and Noah Lucas (Albany: SUNY Press, 1995), 78–79, https://books.google.co.il/books?id=iVJR9UZnTVAC&pg=PA58&redir_esc=y#v=onepage&q&f=false.

15 Indeed, the Sabbath was ultimately defined as the day of rest in social legislation. See below, p 24.

16 Under the Mandate (as previously under the Ottoman regime), marriage law was a matter of a person's (mandatory) affiliation with a religious community and its law. See, e.g., Simcha H. Miron, "The Special Court under Article 55 of the King's Order in Council and the Mystery of Its Rareness," *Diné Israel* 10–11 (1980/81–1982/83): 220–222 and notes) [Heb.].

but no more. The letter ignores a number of issues relevant to religion and state that were already a matter of public debate at the time, such as the question of religious services and who is considered to be Jewish.[17]

Some believe that this document is the origin of the Status Quo,[18] but this view is erroneous. The letter is more of a declaration of intent, presenting a general framework without making any real commitment to Agudat Israel and the Orthodox.[19] It was hardly mentioned in later discussions on the relations between religion and state. However, it was intended to state that the Jewish Agency, as the representative body of the Yishuv, recognized the importance and complexity of these matters and the need for the parties to come to an accord about them. The letter may also reflect the leadership's understanding and acceptance of the main elements of the future relations between religion and state, and as such can be considered to be one of the foundations of the Status Quo.[20]

The Pre-State Legal Arrangements as a Source of the Status Quo

Over the years, there have been ad hoc agreements between the various factions of the Zionist movement, as well as among other groups in the country, about religion-state issues.[21] These agreements were also manifested in legislation and

---

17 The omission may be explained by the fact that at the time Agudath Yisrael did not raise every pertinent issue; the first part of the letter notes that it refers to a specific request related to the four topics covered. Moreover, inasmuch as, before the establishment of the state, immigration was controlled by a foreign power, the ultraorthodox may not have given much thought to the issue. On the question of the Status Quo vis-à-vis recognition as a Jew in the early days of the state, see Eliezer Don-Yehiya, "Religion, National Identity and Politics: The Crisis on the Question of Who Is a Jew—1958," in *Religion and State in Israel, 1948–1967*, ed. Mordechai Bar-On and Zvi Zameret (Jerusalem: Yad Ben-Zvi, 2002), 88 [Heb.]; Aviad Hacohen, "'State of Israel: This is a Holy Place!' The Shaping of the Jewish Public Space in the State of Israel," in Bar-On and Zameret, *Religion and State in Israel, 1948–1967*, 144 [Heb.].

18 The progressive Israeli politician Shulamit Aloni, for example, believed that the letter was the source of the Status Quo. See Shulamit Aloni, *The Arrangement: From a State of Law to a State of Halakhah* (Tel Aviv: Otpaz, 1970), 90. See also Prager, "This Is the History."

19 For a similar analysis, see Friedman, "The History of the Status Quo," 51–52.

20 For more on the religion-state debate in the first years of statehood, see: Zvi Zameret, "A Jewish State, Yes: A Clerical State, No. The Leaders of Mapai and Their Attitude Towards Religion and the Religious," in Bar-On and Zameret, *Religion and State in Israel, 1948–1967*, 175; Hacohen, "The Shaping of the Jewish Public Space."

21 Ehud Luz has described the fierce struggles between the ultraorthodox, the mainstream Orthodox, and the other streams about the Zionist movement's character and its attitude towards religion. He also described the rabbis' opposition to the movement when it became clear that it was completely secular in nature and that "the desecration of the Holy Land was

in voluntary arrangements, usually on the local level, by the Jewish community of Mandatory Palestine.

Consequently, another important source for the Status Quo is the Law and Administration Ordinance 5708-1948.[22] Article 11 of the ordinance incorporated all laws in effect in the country before the establishment of the state, with the necessary modifications due to independence, into the new body of Israeli law.[23] The idea was to avoid a legal vacuum until such time as the country could enact its own legislation.

Even before independence, Zerach Warhaftig,[24] one of the drafters of the Law and Administration Ordinance,[25] had already noted the problems posed by religion-and-state arrangements from a political and constitutional standpoint. Hence he proposed that in these matters the country abide by the Status Quo.[26] In a memorandum setting forth the basic guidelines he considered appropriate for the laws of the state,[27] he took up the matter:

> It should be noted that one of the important problems of the future constitution is the regulation of the relations between

---

being realized in Israel." See Ehud Luz, *Parallels Meet: Religion and Nationalism in the Early Zionist Movement, 1882–1904*, trans. Lenn J. Schramm (Philadelphia: The Jewish Publication Society), 127.

22 Ron Harris believes that the Law and Administration Ordinance played a crucial role in shaping the relations between religion and state in Israel. See: "Absent-Minded Misses and Historical Opportunities: Jewish Law, Israeli Law and the Establishment of the State of Israel," in Bar-On and Zameret, *Religion and State in Israel, 1948–1967*, 21, 26–28; Friedman, "The History of the Status Quo" concurs.

23 Section 11 of the Law and Administration Ordinance stipulates that "The law which existed in Palestine Israel on the 5th Iyar, 1708 (14th May, 1948) shall remain in force, insofar as there is nothing therein repugnant to this Ordinance or to the other laws which may be enacted by or on behalf of the Provisional Council of State, and subject to such modifications as may result from the establishment of the State and its authorities" (official translation at http://www.knesset.gov.il/review/data/eng/law/kns0_govt-justice_eng.pdf).

24 Dr. Zerach Warhaftig of the Mizrachi movement headed the Law Department of the Va'ad Leumi (National Council), and in this framework he struggled to draft a constitution for Israel and wrote two memoranda in which he proposed the basis of the constitution. See Friedman and Radzyner (*supra* note 25), 37; Warhaftig, *Constitution*, 22. He was later one of the signatories on the Proclamation of Independence, a member of the Provisional Council of State, and a long-time government minister.

25 Radzyner, "Forgotten Foundations," 121.

26 As a result, some see Warhaftig as the father of the Status Quo. See Eliezer Don-Yehiya, *The Politics of Regulation: Settlement of Religious Disputes in Israel* (Jerusalem: Floersheimer Institute for Policy Studies, 1997, 32–33) [Heb.].

27 The memorandum bears the date October 30, 1947, meaning that it was written before the UN General Assembly voted for partition and the establishment of a Jewish state but after the Status Quo Letter (dated June 19 of that year).

> religion and state, not only with regard to the national minorities, but also with regard to Jewish life itself. To our joy, these problems can be resolved, to a greater or lesser degree, without excessive shocks. The most important religious problems that require a constitutional arrangement are: the problem of observance of a day of rest—the Sabbath; marital and personal status legislation, including regulations of the affairs of religious trusts; and the organization of the communities and the rabbinate. It is reasonable and acceptable that in all these matters, the guarantee of the "Status Quo" will be the desired solution.
>
> Rest on the Sabbath. . . . Most of the constitutions in the world guarantee a day of rest. . . . Of course, in a constitution matters can be guaranteed only in general; the details are part of the Sabbath law that will be adopted later.
>
> Regarding family legislation and personal status, including the rabbinical jurisdiction as currently exists, the constitution must ensure the perpetuation of this legal situation. Any change whatsoever in this situation is liable to cause serious problems at the start of the building of the Jewish state and lead to undesirable public tremors. . . . Given the liberal nature of Jewish religious law in the area of family and personal status legislation, and noting the natural tendency ingrained in broad strata of Jews to maintain the traditional form in these vital matters, we need not expect any opposition by major circles to the aforementioned arrangement.[28]

Warhaftig, who recognized the difficulties and conflicts related to issues of religion and state, and expected them to intensify as independence approached, already viewed the Status Quo as a comfortable escape and a way to avoid a decision on these issues. As he explained later,

> [i]n the constitutional memoranda I composed and circulated as the director of the Law Department of the National Council . . . I proposed principles for regulating the problems of religion and state. . . . I defined the arrangement I proposed as one of maintaining the existing situation, "the Status Quo." I employed a definition that is accepted by many who want to encourage the

28 Warhaftig, *Constitution*, 442.

> nation in its difficult battle to consolidate the nation so that it can withstand the great battles that lie before it.[29]

In other words, the immediate need for social unity made it preferable to retain the existing situation and postpone decisions about the matter until a later time.

Indeed, among other things, the legislation in force during the Mandate regulated the marital status of Jews and specified that this would be in accordance with Jewish religious law,[30] (indirectly) regulated the Jewishness of a person who wished to convert,[31] set the rules for the weekly day of Sabbath rest,[32] and provided for religious services.[33] These laws, which were originally incorporated en bloc into Israeli law, were modified in part in the early years of statehood; the new laws coalesced into the Status Quo. The best example of an arrangement that predates the state and was modified after its establishment is the Rabbinical Courts (Marriage and Divorce) Law, 5713-1953, which gave the rabbinical courts exclusive jurisdiction regarding the marriage and divorce of Jews in Israel.[34]

Customary Practice and Implicit Agreements

Some elements of the Status Quo scheme derive from understandings that became customary practice but whose origins and source of authority are difficult to pinpoint. It is clear, however, that respect for current practices led to a tacit agreement that maintained them for a while.[35] For example, not every aspect of the Status Quo with regard to the Sabbath is anchored in legislation;

---

29 Ibid., 64.

30 In Articles 51, 53, and 59 of the Order of the King in Council, which were the basis for the regulations for religious court procedures enacted by the self-governing authority of the Yishuv (Knesset Yisrael) in 1928.

31 The Religious Community (Conversion) Ordinance of 1927 stipulates that the head of each religious community in the country must approve a conversion for it to have legal validity, authority, and that the chief rabbi is the head of the Jewish religious community.

32 Sabbath observance was regulated by secondary (local) legislation, because the high commissioner objected to primary (countrywide) legislation on the subject. In 1947, eighteen local councils had Sabbath bylaws in effect.

33 The Religious Communities (Organization) Ordinance of 1926.

34 This law brought some order into the previous situation. See below, p. 47.

35 On the politics of consensus, see Asher Cohen and Baruch Zisser, "Between a Fragile Consensus and Fracturing the Consensus: Changes in the Religion-State Relations, from Consociationalism to Decision," in *Multiculturalism in a Democratic and Jewish State: Ariel Rosen-Zvi Memorial Volume*, ed. Menachem Mautner, Avi Sagi, and Ronen Shamir (Tel Aviv: Ramot, 1998), 675–678 [Heb.].

some simply stem from "what was done." The clearest example is the ban on the operation of public mass transport on the Sabbath (except in Haifa and Eilat), for which there was not clear statutory basis until 1992.

Another element of the Status Quo that was based on an unspoken agreement is the determination of "who is a Jew." It is true that the issue was debated even before the establishment of the state and in its early days, but there was a general consensus that in the immediate aftermath of the Holocaust it should be set aside. So when the Law of Return was passed in 1950, the religious factions did not object to its inclusion of many persons who were not Jewish by religious law and no real attempts were made to define who is a Jew for other purposes.[36] According to Warhaftig, at the time it was clear to him and his colleagues that there was an understanding that a Jew was a Jew only as defined by halakhah[37] (although even then some disputed this).[38] These and other nebulous agreements created norms that came to be perceived as part of the Status Quo, and both the Knesset and the courts took them into consideration when they dealt with the matter.

The Starting Points of the Status Quo

The Status Quo is amorphous. The many areas it covers and the complex arrangements that apply to some issues make it very difficult to point to the full set of balancing acts that together constitute the Status Quo. Another aspect that must be taken into account when we try to describe the Status Quo is what year we have in mind. Leaving aside the modification of the Status Quo on certain issues, some issues were not viewed in this context because they had not yet come up or because there was no awareness of a religious-secular disagreement about them (for example, the subject of human remains and of graves uncovered by archaeological excavations). This means that the Status Quo must always be seen as a snapshot of the situation, from a certain angle and at a particular point in time. This implies that there can be many pictures of the Status Quo, which vary as a function of time and perspective.[39] In order to measure the erosion of the Status Quo on the key issues, then, we must begin by looking at the starting point of the Status Quo as it applies to each issue on its own.

---

36 This was finally done in 1970, after bitter struggles.

37 Warhaftig, *Constitution*, 154.

38 The question came up when the Law of Return was enacted. But Ben-Gurion, aware of the great sensitivity of the matter, preferred not to deal with it in the early years of statehood. See Don-Yehiya, "Religion, National Identity and Politics," 90–93.

39 Michael Corinaldi, "Freedom of Religion in Israel: How Has the Status Quo Changed?" *Sha'arei Mishpat* 3 (2003): 287–330 [Heb.].

3

The Erosion of the Status Quo

The Status Quo began its public and legal path as a series of laws and political agreements, created at different times, which eventually coalesced into a complex system. Over the years it has changed, altered its form, and sometimes expanded. But in the past three decades, and even more so in recent years, it seems to have been eroding, losing both content and relevance.

Several factors have led to this erosion. 1) With regard to demographics, the Jewish population of Israel has grown dramatically, and the composition and numerical ratios among the various sectors (in contemporary language, the "tribes")[1] that compose it have changed. On the one hand, those with a traditionist identity now constitute a majority of the Jewish population; on the other hand, the ultraorthodox community has grown as well.[2] 2) With regard

1 The terms used by the president of Israel, Reuven Rivlin, to define the four main communities that compose Israeli society today: secular Jews, religious Jews, ultraorthodox Jews, and Arabs (Reuven Rivlin at Herzliya Conference, June 7, 2015, https://www.gov.il/he/Departments/news/speech-140616-01.

2 In 1948 the ultraorthodox accounted for about 2% of the adult population of Israel, whereas today the figure is approximately 13%. See Lee Cahaner, Gilad Malach, and Maya Choshen, *The Yearbook of Ultra-Orthodox Society in Israel 2021* (Jerusalem: The Israel Democracy Institute and the Jerusalem Institute for Policy Studies, 2021]), 11. On secularism and traditionalism in Israeli society, see Shmuel Rosner and Camil Fuchs, *Israeli Jewry: A Portrait of a Cultural Revolution* (Modi'in District: Kinneret Zmora Bitan Dvir, 2018), 51, 80, 226 [Heb.].

to Israeli society, many changes have taken place in the seventy years since the birth of the Status Quo. The Israel of the late 1940s and early 1950s, when most of the religion and state arrangements were instituted, was very different from the Israel of 2020. The set of normative values shifted as the relations among its Jewish identity, national character, and democratic nature changed. Israel today is more open, more liberal, and more globally oriented than in the past.[3] 3) Along with the change in values, there has been a shift from an ethical society to one largely based on consumerism and materialism.[4] 4) Over the years the Supreme Court has become more activist and sometimes finds itself compelled to greater intervention in matters of religion and state. In fact, most of the significant changes in religion-state arrangements have been the result of its rulings. 5) Civil society, including organizations that seek to introduce greater pluralism to the expression of Judaism in the public sphere and in legal arrangements, has become much more active in the past three decades.[5] 6) There has also been a change in the degree of involvement and interest shown by non-Orthodox Israelis in the religious services they consume, largely due to the awareness raised by various organizations. In addition to working to change policy, some of these organizations offer religious services that compete with those recognized by the state.[6] 7) Over the years, the tribalization of Israeli society has become more prominent and the demographic segregation of towns and neighborhoods as predominantly secular/religious/ultraorthodox has grown. 8) As a result, the local influence on and control of practices and regulations has come to rival those on the *national level.*

To demonstrate how the Status Quo has crumbled, I will examine four central issues that are the main irritants for those who feel burdened by its arrangements: Sabbath observance in the public sphere, marriage and divorce,

---

3 Ben-Porat, *Between State and Synagogue*, 64–65.

4 Oz Almog, *The Sabra: The Creation of the New Jews*, trans. Haim Watzman (Berkeley and Los Angeles: The University of California Press, 2000), 136; Ben-Porat, *Between State and Synagogue*, 109–113.

5 See Benny Gidron, Nissan Limor, and Ester Zychlinsky, *From Third Sector to the Civil Sector: On the Collective Identity of Civil Society Organizations* (Jerusalem: Van Leer Jerusalem Institute, 2015), 16 [Heb.]; Nissan Limor, *Civil Society and the Third Sector in Israel* (Jerusalem: The Israel Democracy Institute, Caesarea Economic Policy Planning Forum, 2010), 18 [Heb.].

6 For example, Zohar and the organization of liberal Orthodox rabbis have established a kashrut supervision department that will compete with the service offered by the Chief Rabbinate of Israel (see Yaki Adamker, "Tzohar Rabbis Announce a Kashrut System that Competes with the Rabbinate: We Accepted the Challenge," *Walla!* Feb. 26, 2018 [Heb.], https://news.walla.co.il/item/3138477).

conversion (who is a Jew), and kashrut.[7] For each of them I will look at the original arrangement, the changes over the years, and the erosion as a result of alternative legal arrangements that effectively empty it of content.

2.1 The Sabbath

Introduction

Of all the religion-state issues, that of the Sabbath is the most loaded. Already in the infancy of the Zionist movement it troubled the leaders of religious Zionism, the ultraorthodox, and the other factions.[8] From then until the present, there has been a bitter debate about the meaning of the Sabbath as a day of rest, at times so acute as to earn the designation of the "Sabbath Wars."[9]

Today, the character of the Sabbath in the public domain Israel rests on three pillars: the countrywide arrangements, based on the Hours of Work and Rest Law; local regulation by means of municipal bylaws; and practice. The Sabbath legislation and regulations impose various prohibitions on economic and transportation activity on the Sabbath (as detailed below), thereby infringing individual rights and freedoms: (1) The ban on employing Jewish workers and engaging in commercial activity on the Sabbath infringes the freedom of occupation of business owners and workers who wish to work on this day.

---

7 As noted previously (p. 9.), there are additional issues that can be defined as part of the Status Quo and for which the picture is similar. For example, Daphne Barak-Erez, in her detailed account of the evolution of the statutory ban on raising and selling pork and the status of the prohibition today, detects an erosion from the starting point of the Status Quo; see Daphne Barak-Erez, *Laws and Other Animals: Religion, State and Culture in the Light of the Law of the Pig* (Jerusalem and Ramat Gan: Keter and Bar-Ilan University, 2015), 145 [Heb.].

8 According to the Jewish law, Shabbat starts on Friday afternoon and ends on Saturday night. Luz, *Parallels Meet*, 231–241.

9 An instructive example is the "Sabbath wars" in the early days of Tel Aviv (see Ilan Shchori, "The Sabbath War in Tel Aviv," My Tel Aviv, accessed Jul 20, 2022, http://www.mytelaviv.co.il/Shabat-BetelAviv [Heb.]). The announcement published by the municipality in August 1933, over the mayor's signature, in which he calls on the citizens of Tel Aviv and visitors to preserve the sanctity of the Sabbath, not to travel in the city in cars and buses, and to close stores on the Sabbath (see ibid.) is very interesting. A few recent examples: "The Sabbath War in Israeli Football," *Walla!*, August 8, 2017, http://sports.walla.co.il/item/2888824; Ayala Chananel, "Sabbath War in Jerusalem: 14 ultraorthodox Arrested," *Walla!* Aug. 29, 2009, http://news.walla.co.il/item/1545736; Nurit Kadosh, "The Sabbath War: The Supermarkets in Tel Aviv Remained Open and Were Fined," *Calcalist*, July 5, 2014 [Heb.], http://www.calcalist.co.il/marketing/articles/0,7340,L. This issue, like so many others, is highly politicized. Here, though, I focus on the legal arena and how this struggle has been and still is expressed in legislation and court rulings.

(2) The ban on commerce impairs consumers' freedom to shop on the Sabbath and engage in recreational activities of their choice. (3) The general cessation of public transportation on the Sabbath severely impairs citizens' freedom of movement.[10] (4) The closure of streets on the Sabbath has a similar, if lesser, effect. (5) All of the Sabbath-related restrictions can be perceived as infringing the freedom from religion of those who do not attach religious value to the Sabbath.[11] (6) On the other hand, in some cases activities on the Sabbath can be perceived as infringing on the freedom of religion. (7) Finally, the Sabbath, with its positive and negative observances, is a central value of Judaism and thus of the Jewish state.

After describing the starting point of the Status Quo on the Sabbath,[12] I will show that there has been a significant erosion over the years, to the point that even the current legislation on the matter is not enforced and many commercial centers and factories that were formerly shuttered on the Sabbath now operate seven days a week.

The Origins of the Sabbath Status Quo during the British Mandate

Under the Mandate, the leaders of the nonobservant majority recognized the national value of the Sabbath and consequently the importance of Sabbath as the day of rest for the People of Israel who were returning to their land.[13] This recognition, together with the constant efforts of the religious parties and movements,[14] led to attempts to have the Mandatory authorities define Saturday as the day of rest for the Yishuv. These proved unsuccessful, however, because the British high commissioner rejected such a law as incompatible with Article 15 of the League of Nations Mandate for Palestine and Article 63 of the

10 See below, p. 43.

11 HCJ 174/62, The League for the Prevention of Religious Coercion v. the Jerusalem City Council, P. D. 16 (4) 2665 (1962).

12 For an interim summary of the legislation relating to the Sabbath, see Zerach Warhaftig, Haim Hefetz, and David Glass, eds., *Religion and State in Legislation: A Collection of Legislation and Rulings* (Jerusalem: Ministry of Religious Affairs, 1974), 179 [Heb.].

13 An interesting example of this can be found in a special clause that the Jewish National Fund (JNF), the legal landowner, included in its contracts with agricultural settlements. See Yossi Katz, "Religion and Zionism in the Yishuv Era: The Sabbath-Observance Clause in Lease Contracts between the Jewish National Fund and the Agricultural Settlements," *Zion* 78, no. 2 (2013): 207–236 [Heb.]

14 Mainly Mizrachi and Hapoel Hamizrachi, the two religious Zionist movements.

Order in Council, which guaranteed freedom of religion and conscience for the inhabitants of Palestine. According to Warhaftig, the high commissioner feared that such a law would be an expression of the bond between the Jewish people and the country and thus tilt the balance against the Arabs.[15]

Because this meant that that no countrywide Sabbath law would be enacted, the Yishuv found an alternative solution: several localities passed municipal bylaws to require the closure of businesses on the Sabbath, as they were empowered to do under section 98 of the Municipalities Ordinance. Tel Aviv was the first to follow this path, in 1937, and was followed by other towns and local councils. By 1948, such bylaws were in effect in eighteen localities.

These bylaws were supplemented by a number of accords and customary practices, including the cessation of public transportation[16] and the closure of Jewish public institutions on the Sabbath (i.e., from just before sundown on Friday until nightfall on Saturday). On these issues, the consensus reached by the Yishuv and Zionist movement over the years was incorporated into the Status Quo as its cornerstone.

Sabbath Work Restrictions on the Countrywide Level

As we have seen, the Status Quo Letter included the explicit commitment that the Sabbath would be the day of rest in the future state, but did not define the matter any further. As the end of the mandate approached, a committee of jurists (the Law Department of the Va'ad Leumi) was formed to discuss the elements of the constitution and legal system of the future state. Its director, Zerach Warhaftig, endeavored to draft a constitution that would include explicit provisions regarding the Sabbath; other proposals, too, mentioned the Sabbath, while some remained silent on the subject.[17]

In the end, time ran out and the country was proclaimed without a constitution;[18] the Provisional Council of State made do with the Law and

---

15 Warhaftig, *Constitution*, 264.

16 Asher Cohen and Baruch Zisser, *From Acceptance to Escalation: The Religious-Secular Divide at the Beginning of the Twenty-First Century* (Jerusalem and Tel Aviv: Schocken, 2003), 53 [Heb.].

17 The Sabbath was mentioned in the documents submitted to the Law Department by Dr. Pinchas Cohen, Dr. Werner Freistetter, and Dr. Itamar Freund, and by the Mapai party proposal (where the topic was mentioned in the section on workers' rights). It was ignored in the draft prepared by Dr. Shmuel Rolbant. See Warhaftig, *Constitution*, 67. See also Friedman and Radzyner, *The Religious Community and the Constitution*, 38–44.

18 Because no consensus could be reached on many issues (especially those of religion and state), it was decided to postpone the drafting and ratification of a constitution to a later date. See ibid.

Administration Ordinance, whose text made no mention of the Sabbath. Warhaftig, who was trapped in besieged Jerusalem when it was enacted, made vigorous efforts to rectify the matter; the result was the Days of Rest Ordinance 5708-1948, which was retroactively inserted in the Law and Administration Ordinance as section 18a. But even this amendment states only that the Sabbath and Jewish holidays will be days of rest, without defining their character further.[19] That had to wait for passage of the Hours of Work and Rest Law.[20]

The Hours of Work and Rest Law: Social Legislation or an Establishment of Religion?

The Hours of Work and Rest Law 5711-1951[21] is the statutory basis for the Sabbath restrictions in Israel.[22] The law is classic social legislation; until recently it did not specify any specifically religious element of Sabbath observance, but only that Saturday was defined as the weekly day off for Jewish workers.[23] The explanatory notes to the law state this clearly; they say nothing about the Sabbath as a key Jewish value and state that the purpose of the law is to comply with international conventions[24] that deal with workers' rights.[25] In addition, the law did not apply to certain sectors, such as members of cooperatives and

---

19 This ambiguity was intentional (see Hacohen, "State of Israel," 156–157, 165).

20 On this development, see also Gideon Sapir, "And You Will Call the Sabbath Pleasure? Work, Commerce, and Entertainment on the Sabbath in Israel from the Establishment of the State to the Present," *Bar-Ilan University Law Studies* 2 (2018): 583–648.

21 The Hours of Work and Rest Law, 5711-1951. English translation at http://www.ilo.org/dyn/natlex/docs/ELECTRONIC/36146/81476/F1584867301/ISR36146.pdf.

22 The law was amended in 1969 and its application expanded. See below.

23 The only slight reference to the Sabbath in its religious sense is found in §8 of the law, which stipulates that the weekly day off will last "no less than twenty-five consecutive hours" (the duration of the Sabbath under religious law).

24 Restrictions on commerce and economic activity on the weekly day off are found in many countries, although the trend is to a reduction in the scope of the prohibitions they mandate. See Tomer Yehud and Ariel Finkelstein, "Trade and Labor Law on the Day of Rest in the Countries of the World," Institute for Zionist Strategies, July 2016, http://izs.org.il/wp-content/uploads/2016/07/%D7%9E%D7%97%D7%A7%D7%A8-%D7%9E%D7%A9%D7%95%D7%95%D7%94-%D7%99%D7%95%D7%9D-%D7%94%D7%9E%D7%A0%D7%95%D7%97%D7%94-%D7%A7%D7%95%D7%91%D7%A5-%D7%A1%D7%95%D7%A4%D7%99.pdf [Heb.].

25 See section 10 of the explanatory notes to the draft Hours of Work and Rest Law, 5750-1950, https://www.nevo.co.il/law_word/Law17/PROP-0043.pdf.

the self-employed.[26] The first Knesset passed the law over the objection of the religious factions.[27] The "Sabbath law" envisioned by the latter even before the establishment of the state, and even more so afterwards, would have been a declaration by the Jewish state of the sanctity of the Sabbath. But the law that was finally enacted dealt with the prohibition on work and commerce rather than being an expression of that sanctity. Warhaftig's vision was of a law that would not only preserve the aspect of physical rest but would also reflect the special nature of the Sabbath, as perceived by Judaism, as a day of rest for the soul and of spiritual elevation.[28]

Not only was the law not a "Sabbath law," it also contained clauses that were problematic for the religious parties. Section 12 establishes a mechanism for allowing work on the Sabbath with a special permit issued by the minister of labor and social affairs and cosigned by the prime minister and minister of religious affairs. Section 17 stipulates a 50% higher wage for employees who work during the weekly hours of rest. Section 30 excludes many sectors from its coverage, including some that the religious parties did not believe should enjoy such an exemption. In fact, most of the religious members of the Knesset voted against the law.[29] By contrast, the members of other Knesset factions saw the law as social legislation that also responded to religious needs. In the years that followed it served as an excuse for not passing comprehensive legislation on the Sabbath.

A Comprehensive "Sabbath Law"

Every coalition agreement during the first two decades of statehood included a commitment to the religious factions that the long-awaited Sabbath Law

---

26 When the then–Minister of Labor, Golda Meir, submitted the bill to the Knesset, she said that intention was to guarantee the social rights of workers, as in other countries. She said almost nothing about the Sabbath as a Jewish tradition. Rabbi Levin, the welfare minister, spoke next and emphasized that the law did not address any of the important issues that a Sabbath law should include (see: Knesset Record, 1st Knesset, vol. 9, 1752–1753.

27 In the deliberations by the Knesset Labor Committee, for example, MK Moshe Unna of the United Religious Front expressed his reservations about the law and complained that the law did not reflect the spirit of the Sabbath (session of the Labor Committee, First Knesset, Protocol No. 1, 6 [21 February 1951]).

28 Warhaftig, *Constitution*, 269. See Asher Cohen, "Halakhah and State, Da'at Torah and Politics," in Bar-On and Zameret, *Religion and State in Israel*, 435, 442 [Heb.].

29 MK Avraham-Yehuda Goldrat of the United Religious Front stated in his faction's name: "Every son of Israel who is faithful to God and His Torah will be shaken to the depths of his soul by several clauses in this law. He will see them as a blow to the holy Sabbath, for which our fathers and forefathers gave their lives. . . . In deep pain we realize that the majority of this house is not imbued with this awareness of the holiness of the Sabbath" (*Divrei ha-Knesset*, vol. 9, 1752–1753, 9 Iyar 5711 [May 15 1951]).

would be enacted during the term of the new government.[30] When the seventh government was established after the elections to the third Knesset, in 1955, Ben-Gurion undertook to enact a Sabbath Law;[31] despite that explicit commitment, no bill was drafted. Finally, in 1958, Warhaftig (then deputy minister of religious affairs) submitted a private member's bill to the Knesset. Attorney General Haim Cohen countered with a proposal of a more limited scope.[32] Neither proposal was brought up for a vote and the coalition commitment was not honored.

After the election of the fifth Knesset, conditions were more favorable than ever before for the enactment of the Sabbath Law (as well as other religious laws), due to the parliamentary strength of the National Religious Party and the decline in Mapai's representation. The coalition agreement between the parties for the establishment of the tenth government (August 1961) explicitly stated that a "Rest on the Sabbath and Jewish Holidays Law will be enacted and will apply to businesses (including shows in cinemas and theaters), commercial establishments and stores (except for restaurants), and private and cooperative workshops and industrial plants with salaried and self-employed workers."[33]

Despite this commitment, no Sabbath law was passed during the four years of the Knesset's term. In 1963, Warhaftig, by then minister of religious affairs, submitted to the government the text of a Basic Law: the Sabbath and Jewish Holidays (Prohibition of Commercial Activity) Law.[34] When Labor Minister Yigal Allon objected to the bill, a committee was established, including Warhaftig, Transport Minister Yisrael Bar-Yehuda, and others (known as the Kargman Committee after its chairman, Mapai MK Yisrael Kargman) and tasked with drafting a bill for presentation to the government. This committee drew up two alternative versions, which fulfilled some, but not all, of Warhaftig's demands.[35] On the basis of these proposals, the Sabbath and Jewish Holidays Rest bill, which included a ban on theatrical performances and movie shows, was submitted to the Knesset with the support of the government. Once again,

---

30 See Warhaftig, *Constitution*, 266.

31 Ibid.

32 Cohen's proposal was silent with regard to public transportation on the Sabbath, even though the Status Quo was that it did not operate on Saturdays or holidays (apart from Haifa and Eilat). See "The Rest on the Sabbath and Jewish Holidays Law: Proposals, Documents and Documents" (Jerusalem: Ministry of Religious Affairs, 1965), 10–12 [Heb.].

33 Warhaftig, *Constitution*, 268.

34 Sabbath Rest Law (*supra* note 32), 10–12.

35 The sequence of events can be traced back to the exchange of letters among Minister of Religious Affairs Warhaftig, Justice Minister Dov Joseph, Minister of Labor Yigal Allon, their legal advisers, and the Prime Minister's Bureau (see "Religious Laws," Yad Levi Eshkol Archive, P-7/4802).

Allon objected, and while his appeal was being considered the Knesset's term ended and the bill died with it.[36]

The Amendment to the Hours of Work and Rest Law

In 1966 Allon resubmitted his proposal (originally offered near the end of the fifth Knesset) to the new government established after the election of the sixth Knesset, this time as an amendment to the Hours of Work and Rest Law. This proposal included an extension of the prohibition on work to the self-employed in their own businesses and to members of cooperatives (section 9a of the Hours of Work and Rest Law):

> (a) On the prescribed days of rest, within the meaning of the Law and Administration Ordinance 5708-1948, the owner of a workshop or industrial plant shall not work in his workshop or plant and the owner of a shop shall not do business in his shop.
>
> (b) On the aforesaid days of rest, a member of a cooperative society shall not work in a workshop or industrial plant belonging to the society; a member of an agricultural cooperative society shall not work in a workshop or industrial plant belonging to the society unless the work is connected with the services necessary for its farm.[37]

The proposal did not even partially satisfy the demands of the religious factions in the Knesset; some religious MKs insisted that the Knesset should not permit by law what was prohibited by the Torah.[38] In any case, the amendment confirmed the social component of the law[39] insofar as the restriction was applied to another economic sector in a way that preserved its rights and did not recognize competing religious values.[40]

---

36 Warhaftig, *Constitution*, 267–270.

37 The Hours of Work and Rest (Amendment) Law, 5729-1969 (*Sefer ha-Hukim* 5729, 54).

38 This argument is frequently raised by rabbis and ultraorthodox Knesset members in opposition to any bill that contains a compromise on religious matters. This time it was MK Avraham Verdiger (Po'alei Agudat Yisrael) who brought it up.

39 In March 1969.

40 Explaining the bill to the Knesset before it voted, Allon said that "The bill before you seeks to determine that the norm of a day off on the Sabbath and Jewish holidays for employees in workshops and industry will also apply to the self-employed and to members of cooperatives in those sectors. Likewise, commerce in stores will be forbidden. . . . It is hereby proposed to

In early 2018, the Hours of Work and Rest Law was again amended under the pressure of the ultraorthodox parties. The amendment allows the minister of labor, who is empowered to grant Sabbath work permits, to take account of "Jewish tradition."[41] Here at last was a statute that recognized the religious context of the Sabbath. However, no law has been enacted that directly regulates economic activity on the Sabbath[42] or that defines the Sabbath restrictions on a national level and in a coherent manner.

The religious parties did not support the law of Work Hours and Rest because they did not see it as a satisfactory solution. But after it was enacted and it became clear that it reduced economic activity on the Sabbath, they saw its enforcement as a tool to enhance public Sabbath observance.[43]

Sabbath Work Restrictions on the Local Level

As mentioned, under the Mandate, Sabbath observance was regulated by municipal bylaws (in eighteen localities by 1948). At independence, the Municipalities Ordinance[44] was incorporated into Israeli law, including the power granted to local authorities by section 98 (23) "to regulate the opening and closing of stores . . . and to determine . . . their opening and closing on any given day." In the subsequent years, a number of additional localities enacted such bylaws.[45]

---

extend the application of the Hours of Work and Rest Law without violating the accepted Status Quo" (*Divrei ha-Knesset*, vol. 46, 2157-2158, 1 Av 5726 [July 18, 1966].

41 *Sefer ha-Hukim* 5778, No. 2675, Dec. 28, 2017, 73.

42 The enabling law was amended in 1992, in reaction to a ruling by of the Jerusalem District. See below.

43 By virtue of this law, the Ministry of Labor and Social Affairs, especially when the portfolio has been held by the Shas party, has deployed Sabbath inspectors to combat the growing violations of the law and desecration of the Sabbath. However, even then the extent of enforcement has varied over the years. See Shuki Friedman and Gilad Wiener, "Employment on the Sabbath: The Current Situation," Israel Democracy Institute, accessed July 1, 2022, https://www.idi.org.il/articles/20379.

44 Municipalities Ordinance 1934.

45 Gilad Wiener and Shuki Friedman, *Shabbat Observance Laws and the Prohibition on Municipal Economic Activity* (Jerusalem: Israel Democracy Institute, 2018) [Heb.].

Interim Summary

Until the early 1980s, despite political clashes, violent public confrontations,[46] and lawsuits challenging the Status Quo,[47] there were no serious changes and the situation was more or less as follows: only very limited commercial activity on the Sabbath; limited leisure and recreational activities; no public transportation in most parts of the country; and street closures only in the heart of religious neighborhoods. The shifts that favored the religious sector included the cessation of El Al flights on the Sabbath;[48] those that increased activity on the Sabbath were the permits for the operation of gas stations, mandated by the courts,[49] and broadcasting on the Sabbath by the state television channel.[50] During this period, however, the seeds were sown that enabled the later assault on the Status Quo. The dearth of legislation that clearly defined the boundaries of the activities prohibited on the Sabbath, as well as other factors, contributed to the ambiguity of the Status Quo and its multiple interpretations, which culminated in its substantial erosion.[51]

The Erosion of the Sabbath Status Quo

The turning point in the Sabbath Status Quo came in the mid-1980s. The normative framework of Sabbath observance in the public domain started to be eroded, and there were rampant violations of the law, encouraged by public campaigns waged by secular politicians and activists, and abetted by the

---

46 The Sabbath wars in Jerusalem, for example, began immediately after the establishment of the state, and were so stormy that the military police had to be called in to restore order. See: Zvi Meshi-Zahav and Yehuda Meshi-Zahav, *The Murder of Rabbi Pinchas Segalov: The Sabbath Battles of the Summer of 1956: An Account of the Events and Details . . .* (Jerusalem: self-published, 5743 [1983]), 7; Menachem Friedman, "Neturei Karta and the Sabbath Demonstrations in Jerusalem in 1948–1950: Background and Processes," in *Divided Jerusalem 1948–1967: Sources, Summaries, Selected Incidents, and Background Material*, Sermons and Ecclesiastes, ed. Avi Bareli (Yad Itzhak Ben-Zvi, 1994), 224 [Heb.].

47 For example, the suit prompted by the refusal to issue Sabbath work permits pursuant to section 12 of the Hours of Work and Rest Law. The court ruled that the law's reference to something "essential" meant "something that life depends on" (HCJ 201/68, Kaminetsky v. Director General of the Ministry of Health, P. D. 22 (2) 1113 (1968).

48 Rafi Mann, "The Sabbath Wars: How El Al's Planes were Grounded," *Footnotes to History* (blog), May 26, 2012 [Heb.], https://rafimann.wordpress.com/.../מלחמות-השבת-כך-קורקעו-מטוסי-אל-על.

49 See Criminal Appeal 217/68, Yizramax Ltd. v. State of Israel, P. D. 22[2], 343 (1968).

50 See HCJ 287/69, Meron v. Minister of Labor, P. D. 24(1), 337 (1970).

51 Don-Yehiya (*supra* note 38), at 46.

national and local authorities' reticence to enforce the relevant laws.[52] Most of the erosion was in the areas of commercial and leisure-time and recreational activities. There was also more public transportation on the Sabbath, chiefly in the form of taxi services and private bus companies, as well as, very recently, services run by some municipalities. As for street closures, the Status Quo has been maintained; if anything, more city streets are now blocked on Friday night and Saturday than in the past, as a result of the increase in the ultraorthodox population.[53]

Commerce and Recreational Activity: Change Pushed from the Bottom

In the early decades of statehood, the Status Quo with regard to commercial activity and entertainment on the Sabbath endured. Since the mid-1980s, though, there has been a significant increase in such activity on the Sabbath, both in cities and especially in the countryside. Hundreds of small shops are now open for business on Saturday, in Jerusalem, Tel Aviv, Ramat Gan, and many other cities, and mayors do not enforce the municipal bylaws that prohibit this activity. Outside the cities, near kibbutzim and other places, tens of thousands of Israelis frequent shopping centers every weekend. In recent years, urban shopping malls are no longer shuttered.[54]

Year after year there are more cultural, recreational, and commercial establishments operating on Saturday. This has led to new buying habits, with many people taking advantage of the Sabbath for shopping. According to a

---

52 Another issue that has been at the center of stormy public debate in recent years, and that symbolizes the erosion of the Status Quo, mainly for the ultraorthodox, is maintenance work by government companies, mainly the Israel Electric Corporation and Israel Railways, on the Sabbath. Although this activity is not illegal, because it is done on the basis of permits, the fact that these companies work on the Sabbath vexes the religious and ultraorthodox parties to the point of threatening to leave of the coalition. See Kobi Nahshoni, "The Railway Works on the Sabbath: The Ultraorthodox Threaten to Quit the Government," Ynet, June 19, 2017; Amit Segal, "The Tempest of the Railway Work on the Sabbath: The Ultraorthodox Demand an 'Urgent Meeting' with Netanyahu," *Mako*, Aug. 27, 2016.

53 Data on the extent of street closures on the Sabbath are unavailable. But given the number of neighborhoods and cities (including new neighborhoods and town) populated mainly by the ultraorthodox, the logical conclusion is that more streets are closed on the Sabbath than in the past.

54 See, for example, Zvi Barel, "A Modest Secular Rebellion in Zichron Yaakov," *Ha'aretz*, June 15, 1997; Shahar Ilan, "Petah Tikva Introduces: The Second Sabbath War," *Ha'aretz*, June 15, 1999.

report, 98% of the cinemas, 65% of the museums, 83% of the major cultural institutions, and about 20% of the malls are open on the Sabbath.[55]

A study conducted in 2017 found that about 40% of Israelis shop on the Sabbath—approximately 22% about once a month and others less frequently. The economic incentive for businesses is undeniable; those open on Saturdays report a large increase in their weekly turnover. Commercial centers that operate on Saturdays have more traffic on Saturday nights and Sundays.[56]

The erosion of the traditional Sabbath and increased business activity are unmistakable. Tel Aviv has enacted a bylaw permitting the operation of some shops on the Sabbath (see below). In Kfar Sava, a shopping mall began opening on Saturdays in 2017; the public campaign to close it failed.[57] In Jerusalem, a new cinema complex that operates on Friday night and Saturday opened in 2017. The efforts by the leaders of the local ultraorthodox community to thwart the move failed miserably.[58] In fact, despite the very large ultraorthodox population and tradition of Sabbath observance in the city, and decades of conflict, there is now extensive entertainment and commercial activity on the Sabbath in Jerusalem.[59]

Court Rulings

The erosion may be said to have begun with the opening of the Heichal Cinema in Petah Tikva on Friday nights in 1984. The city had a municipal bylaw prohibiting the operation of places of entertainment on the Sabbath, which the mayor at the time, Dov Tavori, wanted to repeal. Consequently he supported the owners' decision to open the cinema on the Sabbath and did not send municipal inspectors to enforce the law. A bitter ideological campaign ensued and lasted for three years, including demonstrations and violent confrontations, but to no

---

55 Ariel Finkelstein, *The Sabbath in Israel: A Case Study* (Jerusalem: The Institute for Zionist Strategies, 2016), 4 [Heb.]; Nadav Eliash, Eyal Berger, and Ariel Finkelstein, *The Israeli Sabbath: A Proposal to Regulate the Status of the Sabbath in Israel in the Spirit of the Gavison-Medan Covenant* (Jerusalem: The Institute for Zionist Strategies, 2014) 36ff. [Heb.].

56 See Adi Dovrat-Mezrit and Moti Basok, "They're Busy in the Middle of the Week: How Many Israelis Are Shopping on the Sabbath?," *TheMarker*, January 30, 2017 [Heb.].

57 See Alon Schneiderman, "The Mall of the Dispute: The Sabbath Wars Have Kfar Sava, Too," *TheMarker*, Aug. 5, 2016 [Heb.].

58 See "Opening the Yes Planet Multiplex on Saturday in the Capital Will Turn Jerusalem into Tel Aviv," *Walla!* Aug. 14, 2015.

59 Nir Hasson, "The Secularists Won the Battle over the Sabbath; The Campaign Continues," *Ha'aretz*, Aug. 7, 2015.

avail.[60] The cinema remained open even though the municipal bylaw[61] was not amended or repealed.[62]

The local efforts to permit entertainment venues to open on the Sabbath soon bore fruit. In 1987, in the Kaplan case,[63] three partners who operated a cinema in Jerusalem on the Sabbath were prosecuted for violating a municipal bylaw, but were acquitted by the local affairs court. The judge, Ayala Procaccia, ruled that the bylaw's ban on the operation of places of entertainment was invalid because it contradicted the spirit of section 9a of the Hours of Work and Rest Law and the bylaw was null and void. In her opinion, the bylaw was also unreasonable as an inherent violation of individual freedom. Her verdict shows that she gave greater weight to the individual's right to "freedom in matters of religion and faith,"[64] which is infringed when one is forced not to work on the Sabbath, than to the religious value of Sabbath rest: "This provision [the ban on the operation of places of entertainment] constitutes unnecessary interference with civil rights and a substantive violation of the basic rights of a secular population."

Procaccia ruled that section 249 (20) of the Municipalities Ordinance did not empower the municipality to enact bylaws that affect the character of life in the city. It followed that the sections of the Jerusalem Bylaw (Opening and Closure of Businesses) 5715-1955 that mandate the closure of businesses on the Sabbath were null and void, because they exceeded the authority of the municipal legislator.[65]

This ruling, along with others that followed it,[66] did not affect the situation on the national level, since each referred to a specific local bylaw. However, it could be cited to justify noncompliance with local bylaws that had not yet been struck down by a court, thereby creating an atmosphere in which other activities incompatible with a "Puritan Sabbath" were legitimized.

---

60 Anonymous, *A Nation that Sanctifies the Seventh Day: The Campaign for the Sanctity of Sabbath in Petah Tikva* (Jerusalem, n.p., 1987) [Heb.].

61 See HCJ 347/84, Petah Tikva Municipality v. Minister of the Interior, P. D. 39(1), 813 (1985), in which the court ruled that a municipal bylaw cannot empower a mayor to decide to open businesses on the Sabbath.

62 See Naomi Gutkind-Golan, "The Heikhal Cinema Affair as a Symptom of the Religious-Secular Relations in Israel of the 1980s," in *Living Together: Religious-Secular Relations in Israeli Society*, ed. Isaiah (Charles) Liebman (Jerusalem: Keter, 1990), 70 [Heb.].

63 Criminal Case (Jerusalem District) 3471/87, State of Israel v. Kaplan, P. D., 5748 (2), 265, 274.

64 Ibid., 271.

65 As mentioned, under the Mandate local authorities were already empowered to enact bylaws regulating Sabbath observance.

66 See, Sundry civil motion (Jerusalem) 3252/99, Uri Gali v. Benny Kashriel (published in *Takdin*, July 26. 1999); see also below.

As a reaction to Procaccia's ruling, in 1990 the Knesset amended the Municipalities Ordinance by adding a section that specifically empowers local authorities to enact bylaws that prohibit the operation of businesses on the Sabbath ("the empowerment clause").[67] This amendment, the result of political pressure exerted by the religious parties, authorized municipalities to pass Sabbath municipal laws. But the Knesset's explicit declaration that municipalities could require the closure of businesses on the Sabbath did not achieve its end. Despite the amendment, the courts found a way to allow leisure activities on the Sabbath even in localities that did not want them.

This was notably the case of Israel Theaters Ltd., in which the Supreme Court allowed the opening of the cinemas in the Sharon Mall in Netanya.[68] The court found that commercial activity on the Sabbath could be seen as part of the fabric of life and the manner in which the Sabbath was spent by some citizens of Israel.[69] Therefore, it ruled, although the Hours of Work and Rest Law is constitutional and meets the test of the reasonable limitation clause, that the minister of labor may exercise his authority and grant Sabbath work permits in the field of commerce in order to mitigate the violation of fundamental rights.[70]

Another ruling that opened the door for commercial activity on the Sabbath related to the law's application to cooperative associations (meaning mainly kibbutzim). In the late 1990s, several kibbutzim built shopping centers on their land and asserted that a lacuna in the Hours of Work and Rest Law permitted them to do so. The Supreme Court ultimately accepted the claim, albeit implicitly, when it held that because a lenient interpretation of the law is possible, the members of the cooperative associations on which it is based could not be convicted.[71] That is, their commercial activity on the Sabbath

---

67 Municipalities Ordinance (Amendment No. 40) 5751-1990.

68 Despite the municipality's unequivocal position that the bylaw was intended to prevent the opening of cinemas within its jurisdiction on the Sabbath, Justice Shamgar exhibited great interpretative dexterity to conclude that the bylaws permits it. Here the court gave precedence to the interest of cultural activity on the Sabbath over the clear political will of the city's residents, as expressed in the municipality's position, thereby making it possible to open businesses on the Sabbath (see HCJ 5073/91, Israel Theaters Ltd. v. Netanya Municipality, 197).

69 HCJ 5026/04, Design 222–Shark Deluxe Furniture Ltd. v. the Head of the Sabbath Labor Permits Unit, Ministry of Labor and Social Affairs, 65 (Nevo, Apr. 4, 2005), in the verdict issued by Justice Procaccia and the obiter.

70 See also Request to File Criminal Appeal 10687/02, Handyman Do It Yourself Ltd. v. State of Israel, P. D. 57 (3) 1 (2003).

71 Request to file a Criminal Appeal 731/07, Kibbutz Tzora Cooperative Association v. State of Israel (Nevo, Mar. 5, 2008).

was actually permitted. The operation of these shopping centers led to the establishment of many more outside the cities, in the jurisdictions of kibbutzim or of regional councils that did not enforce their Sabbath bylaws or simply did not have them.

Partial Enforcement

The failure to enact a comprehensive Sabbath Law to regulate Sabbath observance, on the one hand, and the consequent reliance on several normative layers, on the other, led to the regulatory and enforcement chaos with regard to commerce and leisure activities on the Sabbath. As noted, the framework for Sabbath observance at the national level is the Hours of Work and Rest Law, which prohibits the employment or working of a Jew on the Sabbath but does not bar the operation of a business. Commerce and entertainment venues are regulated at the local level. In many localities,[72] municipal bylaws prohibit commercial activity on the Sabbath, and in some cases leisure activities are also prohibited. As a result, the enforcement of Sabbath observance is divided among a number of agencies. The Hours of Work and Rest Law, with its ban on employing a Jew on the Sabbath, falls into the purview of the Ministry of Labor and its Department of Regulation and Enforcement; the closure of businesses on the Sabbath is left to local authorities. This means that a store that employs Jews on the Sabbath can be fined twice for the same violation. But the national and local levels have something in common when it comes to enforcement: in both cases it is incomplete and often reveals the authorities' conspicuous lack of desire to intervene.

Although it is estimated that over one hundred thousand workers are employed illegally every Saturday,[73] the number of fines imposed on employers and criminal cases opened against them is negligible. This can be gleaned from

---

72 Regional councils are an exception, and many of them do not have bylaws prohibiting commercial activity on the Sabbath (see Gideon Zeira, Oriana Almasi, Itai Fidelman, Uri Tal Spiro, and Flora Koch Davidovitch, *Enforcement of the Provisions Regarding the Opening and Closing of Businesses by Local Authorities*, Knesset Research and Information Center, Feb. 6, 2014, 9 [Heb.]). See also Wiener and Friedman, *Shabbat Observance Laws*.

73 For data on the extent of Jewish labor on the Sabbath and the extent of enforcement, see Friedman and Wiener, "Employment on the Sabbath" (*supra* note 45).

the state comptroller's annual report for 2007[74] and from Ministry of Economy data of recent years.[75]

On the local level, the situation is completely chaotic. While some local authorities strictly prevent the operation of commercial establishments, others have a declared policy of nonenforcement. The enforcement of the bylaws on the subject depends on the identity of the head of the authority, the composition of the municipal coalition, and the pressure exerted on the mayor or council head by those with a vested interest in the matter—the religious community and parties, versus the secular organizations and parties. As a result, even though the Sabbath bylaws of many places are quite similar,[76] in practice every locality has its own Sabbath.[77] In response to a query by the Knesset Research Center, a number of cities responded that they do not enforce the prohibition on commercial activity on the Sabbath (including Eilat, Hod Hasharon, Herzliya, Carmiel, Lod, and Upper Nazareth [now Nof Hagalil]); others said that they enforce it selectively, meaning only where it seriously disturbs residents (Ashdod, Beer Sheva, Petah Tikva). In practice, only cities with a clear religious or ultraorthodox identity replied that they enforce the law strictly and allow no commercial activity on the Sabbath.[78]

This means that de facto—and, given the overt nonenforcement of the bans, de jure—it is possible and even legitimate to operate businesses in most of

---

74 State Comptroller, Annual Report 58 (b) for 2007, Audit of the Ministry of Industry, Trade and Labor, 1134; and the subsequent Knesset debate in the State Control Committee, February 26, 2008, on "A Request for the State Comptroller's Opinion on Non-Enforcement of Labor Laws and Licensing Business (Opening Businesses on the Sabbath)," https://www.knesset.gov.il/mmm/data/pdf/m03360.pdf.

75 Data from the Ministry of Economy, which was in charge of enforcing the Hours of Work and Rest Law until recently, show that in 2013, 2014, and 2015, 230 administrative files and dozens of criminal cases were opened for violations of the law. See *Employment of Workers on the Weekly Day of Rest: Regulation and Supervision of the Issue*, Knesset Research and Information Center, Oct. 12, 2015.

76 These bylaws differ drastically. Except for the amended bylaw in Tel Aviv, most of them broadly formulate the prohibition on commerce and some prohibit the opening of leisure places. In Eilat, for example, the municipal bylaw, Opening and Closure of Businesses, 5737-1977, provides that "2(A) On days of rest, a person shall not open or permit the opening of a restaurant or a business or place of entertainment. (B) Notwithstanding the provisions of subsection (A), on days of rest . . . a person shall be entitled to operate food service where no food or drink is served accompanied by entertainment, music, etc., from the beginning of the day of rest until 22:00. . . . (C) Notwithstanding the provisions of subsection (A), on days of rest . . . a person may open a place of entertainment for the purpose of cultural, educational, and sports activities.

77 Zeira et al., *Enforcement of the Provisions Regarding the Opening and Closing of Businesses*, 15.

78 Ibid., 17ff.

Israel.[79] Although this commercial activity has yet to realize its full potential, the trend is clear and that is only a matter of time.

Sabbath Commerce in Tel Aviv, and Its Ramifications

During the recent years, there has been a significant growth in commercial activity on the Sabbath, which constitutes a precedent for legitimizing it, increasing its scale, and thus to further erosion of the Sabbath Status Quo.

Over the past two decades, convenience store chains have opened many outlets in Tel Aviv, which operate on the Sabbath (alongside the restaurants and cafes that have been doing so for many years). Until the recent amendment of the municipal bylaws (see below), this activity was illegal.[80] Despite this, the municipality enforced the law with a light hand and imposed only moderate fines when it did issue a citation, out of a desire to allow minimarkets, restaurants, cafes, and other businesses to operate for the benefit of residents.

In response to a suit filed by the owner-operators of small grocery stores, the Supreme Court ruled that the municipality must either enforce its bylaw in a way that would end the illegal activity or amend the bylaw.[81] Accordingly, the municipality adopted a new bylaw permitting limited commercial activity, including convenience stores, coffee shops, and all forms of commercial activity, in three defined commercial districts. After three years passed and the interior minister (a member of the ultraorthodox Shas party) failed to countersign the municipal bylaw so that it could take effect, the High Court of Justice ruled twice[82] that the bylaw was valid even without his endorsement.

In her ruling, Court President Miriam Naor opened the door to the creation of diverse local arrangements for business activity on the Sabbath. She noted that the Hours of Work and Rest Law does not prohibit the operation of businesses on the Sabbath, but only the employment of Jews if the employer has not received a permit to do so. As a result, the closure of businesses on the Sabbath is a matter for local authorities to decide. Naor acknowledged the

---

79 On the nature of the workers and work on the Sabbath a decade ago, see Michal Alfasi, "The Hours of Work and Rest Law: Employees Who Work on the Day of Rest," Ministry of Industry, Trade and Labor, Research and Economics Administration, May 2008 [Heb.].

80 Tel Aviv-Yafo Bylaw (Opening and Closure of Stores), 5740-1980; Tel Aviv-Yafo By-Law (Opening and Closure of Stores) (Amendment No. 1), (Amendment No. 2), 5774-2014.

81 Admin. Appeal 2469/12, Bremer v. Municipality of Tel Aviv-Yafo (Nevo, June 25, 2013).

82 HCJ 6322/14, General Association of Merchants and the Self-Employed v. the Minister of the Interior (Nevo, April 19, 2007); HCJ 3660/17, General Association of Merchants and the Self-Employed v. the Minister of the Interior (Nevo, Oct. 26, 2017).

value of maintaining the Sabbath in the public space and the need to balance its observance with the freedom of citizens to spend their day of rest in a way that suits them. She held that the appropriate balance could best be gauged by the local authority:

> The heart of the test is a balance between the conflicting rights. The balance does not favor one worldview over the other. It does not detract, even in the slightest, from the status and importance of the Sabbath as a national asset of the Jewish people and as one of the values of the State of Israel as a Jewish and democratic state, as Ahad Ha'am said: "More than Israel kept the Sabbath, the Sabbath kept them." However, balance means that a thousand flowers will bloom. It means that alongside the protection of the unique character of the Sabbath, each and every individual must be allowed to shape his Sabbath in his own way and according to his beliefs, and to fill it with content as he sees fit. To borrow from [the poet] Zelda, "To light candles in every world—that is the Sabbath" (Zelda, "Sabbath and Weekday"). It was for good reason that the legislature saw fit to assign this balancing act to the local authority. In this way the balancing point chosen will reflect the unique character of each city, its degree of civil coexistence, and the practical solutions that characterize its particular circumstances. Indeed, when the Sabbath arrives, the city dons its festal costume, but the garment donned by one is not the same as the garment of another.[83]

Here Naor proposed a new balance, different from the current one, between the Jewish character of the Israeli public sphere and the rights of individuals to spend the Sabbath in whatever way they feel is appropriate, as well as a balance between the state's role in shaping the public Sabbath by creating an equilibrium between these values, on the one hand, and the role of the local authority, on the other. Naor did not propose parameters for balancing between these interests. She seems to have assigned the local authorities unlimited power to provide residents with a Sabbath experience that suits their preferences. This approach, along with her narrow interpretation of the Hours of Work and Rest Law,

---

83 Ibid., 27.

opens the door for commerce on any scale, despite the camouflage terminology of recognizing the value of the Sabbath. One possible result of the ruling is a race to the bottom by local authorities, avid to please a secular majority and to encourage business owners to operate in their jurisdictions. The ruling, needless to say, represented a significant deviation from the Status Quo that effectively existed in all localities in Israel.[84]

In the wake of this ruling, then Interior Minister Aryeh Deri sponsored an amendment to the Municipalities Ordinance (known as the "Supermarkets Law"), aimed at circumvented the High Court's decision. It stipulates that the authority to approve a municipal bylaw that would permit the opening of businesses on the Sabbath rests with the minister of the interior. Furthermore, the minister's default option is not to approve such a law unless, in his or her opinion, it permits the opening of businesses that are required to "satisfy . . . essential needs."[85] This amendment revived the "Sabbath Wars" but in practice did not really change the existing situation and did not have much effect on the volume of commercial activity on the Sabbath, given that most local authorities already have bylaws that prohibit it on the Sabbath but do not enforce them.

To sum up, the considerable increase in the scale of commercial and leisure activity on the Sabbath is sucking in more and more business, sometimes against their will, and creates the perception that Sabbath is turning into another weekday. So it is not surprising that, according to a recent survey, a large segment of the public supports the expansion of activity on the Sabbath to other domains, such as health clinics and auto repair shops.[86]

---

84 Paragraph 49 of Justice Naor's ruling (ibid.). Justice Daphne Barak-Erez wrote something similar in the first ruling on the petition: "Precisely because of the ethical and practical complexity of the decision on this issue, the Knesset chose to delegate the decision to the local arena, as is made clear in Section 249(20) of the Municipalities Ordinance (New Version). . . . This delegation to the local level does not mean a disavowal of recognition of the uniqueness of the Sabbath. In fact, it expresses a perception that is more than anything else 'Jewish and democratic.' The special and separate regulation of the Sabbath reflects the Jewish national culture (as well as important social values). However, the arrangement includes an important democratic component—democracy at the local level, which permit a more precise expression of the different characteristics of the respective populations of each city" (HCJ 6322/14, 17)72.

85 Municipalities Ordinance, section 258A (*Sefer ha-Hukim*, 5768, No. 2681, Jan. 10, 2018, 110).

86 The data were published in February 2018 as part of the Israel Democracy Institute's "Israeli Peace Index." See the institute's website: https://www.idi.org.il/articles/20734.

Freedom of Movement on the Sabbath

Another central component of the Sabbath Status Quo is the (non)operation of public transportation, and, a somewhat later development, closures of city streets. The situation here is complex, and it is difficult to point to a trend to erosion in the religious or secular direction. However, given several recent initiatives by local authorities to operate public transportation on Sabbath, here too the erosion seems to be in the secular direction.

Public Transportation

The arrangement established at independence, perpetuating the system existing then, was that urban public transportation does not operate on the Sabbath, except in Haifa (and, as the city grew, in Eilat). But this de facto situation was not formalized in law until 1991,[87] when the transportation minister was given the authority to specify bus lines permitted operate on the Sabbath. The guidelines formulated for permitted Sabbath bus lines refer to necessary travel other than the "normal" use of public transportation for leisure and recreational activities.[88] Over the years, the number of lines that operate on the Sabbath has increased, alongside jitneys that run on regular weekday routes. However, the increase in the number of lines operating on Saturdays has not kept pace with the increase in the overall bus system; in any case, a rough estimate is that there has in fact been a per capita decrease in Sabbath bus service. A High Court petition filed in 2017 contended that the state must approve a larger number of lines on the Sabbath, inasmuch as they are a "vital transportation need"; but the court rejected the petition.[89]

---

87 The Traffic Ordinance, section 71 (7a) "prohibits the operation of a public bus on days of rest on a regular line, and for this purpose the Minister shall take into account, as much as possible, the tradition of Israel with regard to the prohibition of the movement of vehicles on days of rest."

88 Section 386 of the Traffic Regulations states that public transportation may be permitted on the Sabbath in specific cases: lines that go to hospitals; lines to border settlements, lines serving non-Jewish communities; and lines that are essential to public security.

89 HCJ 5396/16, Rashap v. Minister of Transport (Nevo, September 11, 2017). The state's response to the High Court of Justice in this case includes data that prove that the increase in the number of permits has not been proportional to the increase in the number of bus lines. However, it is difficult to conclude with certainty that the state changed its policy, because the change ultimately depends on the relevance of the grounds for excluding existing lines compared to the opening of new lines. In its reply, the state also said that in recent years there has been an increase in the number of lines operating on the Sabbath:

Another ongoing change from below can be expected to affect the scale of public transportation on the Sabbath. In recent years, various organizations and municipalities[90] have operated bus lines on the Sabbath; in order to bypass the regulatory requirement of a permit, they operate as cooperative associations or as a free service to their citizens.[91]

Thus, to date the Status Quo has been maintained with regard to public transportation. It can be cautiously predicted, however, that grassroots activity and public pressure,[92] both institutionalized (municipalities) and noninstitutionalized (citizen organizations), will ultimately increase the availability of public transportation on the Sabbath.

Road Closures

Traffic restrictions on the Sabbath existed under the Mandate, and even nonreligious persons favored them. According to a proclamation by the Tel Aviv Municipality, issued in August 1933 and signed by the mayor, Meir Dizengoff, entitled "Against Public Desecration of the Sabbath," "the public buses . . . are requested not to travel on the streets of Tel Aviv on Sabbaths and holidays. . . .

---

164 in 2012, to 383 in 2017. However, an investigation by the business newspaper *Calcalist* found that many lines that have a permit to run on the Sabbath actually infringe on it slightly on Friday afternoons or Saturday evenings and do not really operate on the Sabbath (see Shahar Ilan, "Staying Home: 70% of the Shabbat Lines Don't Actually Run on the Sabbath," *Calcalist*, Sept. 11, 2017).

90 The leaders in this activity are the Herzliya Municipality, which announced the operation of this line (see "The Summer Line on Saturdays and Holidays in Herzliya," accessed July 1, 2022, http://www.herzliya.muni.il/?CategoryID=208&ArticleID=2503) and the Tel Aviv Municipality, which is working on such an initiative. See Gilad Morag, "The Municipality of Tel Aviv Requests: Public on the Sabbath," Ynet, May 5, 2005, http://www.ynet.co.il/articles/0,7340,L-4654173,00.html.

91 The scope of this activity remains limited. Only five such organizations, at various stages of maturity, are currently working to promote public transportation on the Sabbath, but it can be assumed that as demand increases their will be more such activity. See "Public Transportation Lines on Fridays and Saturdays," Hofesh: Freedom from Religion, accessed 1 July, 2022, http://www.hofesh.org.il/alternatives/transp/. See also Nir Hasson, "Bus Service that will Operate on Saturdays Launched in Jerusalem this Weekend," *Ha'aretz*, May 2, 2015, http://www.haaretz.co.il/news/local/1.2627191.

92 Many surveys show that most of the public believes that public transportation should operate on the Sabbath. See "Poll: 72% of the Public Favor Public Transportation on the Sabbath," *NRG*, June 19, 2016. The survey found that even a majority of the religious (52%) support public transportation on the Sabbath; Hillel Poisic, "Smith Institute Survey: 74% of the Public Want Buses on Sabbath," Ynet, Apr. 15, 2015.

All owners of private cars and motorcycles are asked not to travel in the city on Sabbaths and holidays."[93]

After independence, the earliest protest demonstrations against desecration of the Sabbath were against vehicular traffic; most of them were in Jerusalem.[94] A decade later, the normative framework for Sabbath road closures emerged under the Traffic Regulations 5761-1961, which empower a municipal traffic authority to implement traffic arrangements in a particular area, at its discretion. Local authorities have tended to exercise this authority "in easy cases"—neighborhoods and streets where the residents are predominantly religious. Over the years, though, several complex cases have reached the Supreme Court.

As early as 1962, the Jerusalem Municipality used these regulations to close King George Street during Sabbath services at the Yeshurun Synagogue. The High Court turned down a petition against the decision.[95] Justices Shimon Agranat, Zvi Berenson, and Yoel Sussman ruled that avoiding a disturbance to "worshipers gathering" for prayer is a worthy value that must be taken into account, despite the infringement of the full movement of those who use the street.[96]

A similar case occurred in Bnei Brak in 1977. Here too, it was decided to close a section of a main road, this time for the entire Sabbath, because of the sensitivities of the ultraorthodox residents on both sides of the street. Once again the Supreme Court ruled that the balance between the rights of individuals who are prevented from using the road and the rights of ultraorthodox residents whose claim asserts the religious value of Sabbath rest is inclined towards the latter.[97] In both cases the justices evinced little uncertainty and concluded that religious sensitivities may overcome other principles and values.

---

93 Ibid., 24, note 9.

94 Ibid., 32, note 46.

95 HCJ 174/62, The League for the Prevention of Religious Coercion v. The Jerusalem City Council, P. D. 16 2665 (1962).

96 In Jerusalem the issue of traffic on the Sabbath has triggered major conflict between ultraorthodox and secular Jews and led to violent protests by the former, ultraorthodox almost since the establishment of the state. See Friedman (*supra* note 46). In the early 60s there were clashes in Jerusalem about traffic through the ultraorthodox neighborhoods on the Sabbath (see the "Religion" file, Yad Levi Eshkol Archives, 12/4836: Jerusalem District Commander's Report to the Head of the Investigations Department and the District Commander on Violence in the Sabbath in Jerusalem, July 29, 1963; the Southern District Commander's reported to the police commissioner about incidents of throwing stones at cars traveling in the ultraorthodox neighborhoods, October 14, 1963, and a government discussion on Oct. 28, 1963 about the Sabbath demonstrations in Jerusalem and a method to stop them).

97 HCJ 531/77, Baruch v. Traffic Controller in the Tel Aviv and Central Districts Central Traffic Authority, P. D. 32 (2) 160 (1978).

Back in Jerusalem, the Bar Ilan Street case had a different result. In 1996, Transport Minister Yitzhak Levy ordered that this main thoroughfare be closed during the hours of synagogue services on the Sabbath, in recognition of the fact that it runs through a series of heavily ultraorthodox neighborhoods. His decision was appealed to the High Court of Justice;[98] the petitioners argued that closure of the road was a severe violation of the freedom of movement of many residents of the city, as it is a major traffic artery linking neighborhoods, and also that it impairs the ability of secular residents who live nearby to reach their homes on the Sabbath. The court issued an interim injunction to keep the road open, but tried to sidestep this charged matter by calling for the establishment of a public committee (the Zameret Committee) to study the case and submit recommendations. The committee's conclusions were similar to those of an earlier group (the Sturm Committee, appointed in 1994); namely, that it was appropriate to close Bar Ilan Street during Sabbath services. As a result, the minister of transportation again closed the road and the matter was returned to the court. In the end, it made the interim injunction permanent and ruled that the road would remain open for traffic throughout the Sabbath until the minister of transport found a solution that took account of the interests of the secular residents of the predominantly ultraorthodox neighborhoods.

Here the justices, headed by Court President Aharon Barak, arrived at a delicate balance between conflicting values—observance of the Sabbath and respect for religious sensibilities,[99] versus the right to freedom of movement, which is a matter of human dignity. The decision recognized the right of the ultraorthodox to safeguard their religious feelings, but ultimately favored freedom of movement over Sabbath observance as understood by the ultraorthodox residents.[100] Barak wrote that rights deriving from the democratic character of the State of Israel take precedence over—or, if you wish, can erode—its Jewish character. Nevertheless, the ruling legitimized and protected the religious sensibilities and provided a basis for continuation of the policy of

---

98 HCJ 5016/96, Horev v. Minister of Transport, P. D. 51(4) 1 (1997).

99 On the violation of religious sensitivities, see Danny Statman, "Infringement of Religious Sensitivities" in Mautner, Sagi, and Shamir, *Multiculturalism in a Democratic and Jewish State*, 133–188. On freedom of movement as a constitutional right, see Yaffa Zilbershatz, "On Internal Freedom of Movement," *Law and Governance* 4 (1998): 793.

100 This is a simplistic presentation of the matter; the long and complex decision includes a wide range of considerations resulting from a strong awareness of its public sensitivity. However, this is ultimately the balance that the court makes.

closing streets, in particular, and for the protection of religious sensibilities as an important consideration vis-à-vis other rights, in general.

In the more than two decades since this ruling, the issue of road closures in religious neighborhoods and outside synagogues versus the freedom of movement has been another component of public Sabbath observance in Israel and of the Status Quo. In practice, one cannot identify a clear starting point for the Status Quo in this context, because its statutory and regulatory anchors and the extent of the closures have changed over the years.[101] All the same, the principle that roads can be closed when there is a strong religious interest survives today. Measured by the number of roads that are closed, the Status Quo seems to have eroded in the religious direction.[102] But if one takes account of the demographic and geographic expansion of the ultraorthodox and religious sectors, it would seem that the Status Quo remains more or less untouched.

Summary

De facto and de jure, public respect for and observance of the Sabbath have eroded significantly. Commerce on the Sabbath, once the exception, has become the norm in much of the country. The future does not bode for the Jewish cultural, religious, and social values attached to the Sabbath as a day of rest. As more and more stores are open, other merchants have a hard choice to make: between loyalty to their faith, their family, and values, and their reticence to force employees to work, on the one hand, and economic survival, on the other. The political inability to arrive at new arrangements for the Sabbath as a day of rest, the growing momentum of commercial activity on the Sabbath, and local authorities' desire to encourage shopping in their jurisdictions, which has now received statutory legal legitimacy, are all pushing towards Saturdays that will be more like Sundays in America.

---

101 See, for example, Barel, "A Modest Secular Rebellion"; Ilan, "Petah Tikva."

102 I have not been able to locate a quantitative study that accurately measures the change that has taken place regarding this subject. My estimate is based on the increasing number of exclusively ultraorthodox neighborhoods and town. See Gilad Malach, Maya Choshen, and Lee Cahaner, *Annual Report on ultraorthodox Society in Israel 2016* (Jerusalem: Israel Democracy Institute and the Jerusalem Institute for Israel Studies, 2016), 19, 32 [Heb.].

2.2 Marriage and Divorce

Introduction

In Israel, marriage and divorce ("personal status") constitute a complex topic, involving many factors and are tied to two legal systems and two judicial systems.[103] The system that governed personal status in the early days of the state and its subsequent modifications illustrate the ongoing erosion of the Status Quo in this domain as well.[104]

In its most basic form, the regulation of personal status in Israel on the basis of Jewish religious law (halakhah)[105] derived from recognition of the importance of adherence to its rules for the integrity of the Jewish people. However, there are stark contradictions between the personal status prescriptions of Jewish religious law[106] and modern liberal values.[107]

With regard to marriage, the first issue is the many restrictions that halakhah imposes on the very eligibility to marry or to marry the partner of one's choice. The result is that hundreds of thousands of citizens cannot contract a marriage

---

103 Ariel Rosen-Zvi, *Family Law in Israel: The Sacred and the Secular* (Tel Aviv: Papyrus, 1990), 24, 26 [Heb.].

104 The history of marital law in Israel and of the division of powers and struggles between the religious and civil courts and between the rulings of the two jurisdictions is long and complex. In this chapter, I can only present a concise review of its evolution in a way that illustrates the erosion of the Status Quo. For more information, see, e.g., Israel Zvi Gilat, *Family Law: Child-Parent Relations—Alimony, Financial Relations, Child Custody and Education* (Tel Aviv: Hoshen Lemishpat, 2001) [Heb.]. For a later review of developments in marital law in Israel, see Ruth Zafran, "The 'Jurisdiction Race' is Alive and Kicking: Rabbinical Courts Gain Power over Civil Family Courts," *Mishpatim* [Hebrew University law journal] 43 (2013): 571–630 [Heb.]. Since she wrote, additional rulings have tipped the balance towards civil law. In the most recent case, in Family Appeal Request 919/15 and Family Appeal Request 1709/15, Anonymous v. Anonymous (Dec. 6, 2016, shorturl.at/dvz05), the court held that the religious law that imposes alimony and child support on the father, regardless of the mother's financial situation, is unequal. This drastically alters the formula for calculating these payments, with a clear deviation from religious law. See also Daphna Hacker, "Legal Review: What Has Changed This Year? Families' Law between Harmonization and Chaos," *Din Udvarim* 9 (2015): 295–321. [Heb.].

105 For Jews; members of other faiths are subject to their respective religious authorities and laws.

106 It is worth noting that Muslim law, which applies to about one-fifth of the country's citizens, and the laws of other religious groups in Israel, while differing in detail from Jewish law, also contradict a number of key liberal conceptions. For Muslim law, see: Shlomo Dov Goitein and Aaron Ben-Shemesh, *Muslim Law in the State of Israel* (Jerusalem: Hebrew University Student Union, 1957), 213–245 [Heb.]; Yaakov Meron, *Muslim Law in Comparative Perspective* (Jerusalem: Magnes, 2001), chapters 5 and 6 [Heb.].

107 Shahar Lifshitz, "Contractual Regulation of Spousal Relationship in Civil Law" (PhD. diss., Bar-Ilan University, 2002), 505–509.

in Israel. A second issue is that every wedding must be based on a religious ceremony, with its accompanying rituals. The third issue is the inbuilt gender inequality of the wedding ceremony, in which the man plays an active role and the woman remains passive.

Fourth, contrary to the liberal model of marriage, Jewish law defines strict rules, many of them unequal to the detriment of women.[108] When it comes to divorce, the husband has complete control and must actively grant the divorce, unlike the Western norm in which a third party (the civil courts) is vested with the authority to dissolve a marriage, even over the objections of one of the parties. Second, the religious divorce system and the laws surrounding it are based on fault.[109] Third, there is an inherent inequality in property and child-custody rights, favoring the man, in the wake of divorce.

At its birth, Israel was willing to allot the religious values represented by the halakhic family laws a significant place in its overall system of values—even though it was clear that they were inconsistent with liberal principles. But as public awareness of the infringement of individual rights and equality increased, acceptance of the primacy of religious law in this area, with its blatant gender inequality, crumbled. On almost every point mentioned above, there have been changes that reflect liberal values and grant them priority. The last vestige of the exclusivity of religious law relates to divorce, and this too is currently under attack.[110]

The Starting Point of the Status Quo in Marriage and Divorce

With regard to personal status, the Status Quo can be traced to long before statehood.[111] It was based on British Mandatory legislation (which itself continued the situation under the Ottoman Empire) that regulated the personal status of Jews and made them subject to traditional marital law. Within the

---

108 This includes the definition of the husband's and wife's obligations in marriage. See David Yosef Mashilov, "The Jewish Woman in Halakhah," *Diné Israel* 13/14 [1988]: 263.

109 That is, without one of the grounds for divorce specified by halakhah. See Avishalom Westreich, *No-Fault Divorce in the Jewish Tradition* (Jerusalem: The Israel Democracy Institute, 2014), 14 [Heb.].

110 Amnon Rubinstein and Barak Medina, *The Constitutional Law of the State of Israel: Foundations*, 5th ed. (Jerusalem: Schocken, 1996), 195–207.

111 Under the Mandate, personal status was regulated pursuant to Articles 51, 53 and 59 of the King's Order in Council, under whose authority the Yishuv self-governing authority ("Keneset Yisrael") passed regulations in 1928 that governed the procedures and status of the rabbinical religious courts.

Yishuv, there was a broad consensus that this was a domain to be determined by halakhah in order to prevent a schism within the Jewish people. This agreement was reflected in the Status Quo Letter, in the deliberations that preceded independence, and in the subsequent enactment of legislation on the matter.[112]

The Knesset formalized the Status Quo in matters of personal status when it passed the Rabbinical Court Jurisdiction (Marriage and Divorce) Law 5713-1953. According to its first two articles, "(1) Matters of marriage and divorces of Jews in Israel . . . shall be under the exclusive jurisdiction of rabbinical courts. (2) Marriages and divorces of Jews shall be performed in Israeli in accordance with Jewish religious law."[113]

When the law was passed, the religious parties viewed it as a great achievement and an imperative element of the laws of a Jewish state, whose absence would have caused a historic and irreparable rift within the Jewish people. Warhaftig, one of the law's authors, said as much during the Knesset debate that preceded its passage:

> Of the four parts of the *Shulhan Arukh* [the Code of Jewish law] that has guided the lifestyle of the Jewish people and individual Jews for many centuries, the people would not be split apart due to the nonobservance of three of them by some of the people, but who can make amends for [violation of] the fourth. . . .
>
> Non-observance of the *Even Ha'ezer* [the section the contains marital and family law] may result, Heaven forbid, in a schism and rupture that cannot be repaired. A prohibition on marriage [with some prospective spouses would] result in the distancing [of people from one another] at the earliest stage, so that each party does not recognize the other, will not socialize

---

112 Warhaftig, *Constitution*, 179.

113 See the official English text at https://knesset.gov.il/review/data/eng/law/kns2_rabbiniccourts_eng.pdf. In matters of personal status, Muslims, who constitute the second largest religious community in Israel, are subject to the authority of the Shari'a Courts by virtue of the Law and Administration Ordinance, which took over the Mandatory arrangement. The state recognized the appointment of qadis for these tribunals under the Shari'a Courts (Approval of Appointments) Law 5714-1953. The Druze religious jurisdiction is set out in the Druze Courts Law 5723-1962, which is similar to the Rabbinical Court Jurisdiction Law and gives the community's courts explicit authority with regard to marriage and divorce of the Druze in Israel (section 4). The provisions of Mandatory law remain in force for other religions.

> with the another, to the point of complete estrangement, Heaven forbid.[114]

Over the years, this law engendered many problems and became one of the main points of friction between religious values and individual rights. The Knesset and the Supreme Court have slowly chipped away at the rabbinical courts' exclusive jurisdiction as well as the status of religious law as the sole arbiter of marriage and divorce in Israel. Obviously this means a significant erosion in the Status Quo.[115]

The Erosion of the Status Quo on Marriage

The Recognition of Civil Marriage

Halakhah includes various stringencies that define certain men and women as "ineligible to marry" under rabbinic auspices. Because of the rabbis' exclusive jurisdiction, such people cannot wed in Israel and are effectively deprived of the right to marry. In the absence of some form of civil marriage in Israel, the same applies to intermarriages between members of different faiths.[116] In reaction to this problem, over the years the Supreme Court has gnawed away at the exclusive status of religious law by recognizing other forms of contracting a marriage, although still without the existence of civil marriage in Israel.

The Supreme Court first instructed the state to recognize the civil marriage of Jews abroad in its 1963 ruling in the Funk Schlesinger case.[117] The court ruled that Israelis who wed abroad in a civil ceremony must be registered as married in the Population Registry. The High Court held that it sufficed for a couple to produce appropriate evidence, such as a marriage certificate from a foreign country, in order to obligate the registry clerk to register them as married.

---

114 Warhaftig, *Constitution*, 179.

115 To date the Supreme Court has not intervened to issue a divorce or recognize a divorce decreed by a religious court (unlike its ruling on marriage), apparently fearing the implications of such a step or recognizing that it would totally undermine the religious courts (which are on shaky ground in any case).

116 The exception, which is relatively late, is the Civil Union for Citizens with no Religious Affiliation Law 5771-2010, which allows two persons who do not belong to any of the recognized religious communities in Israel to register in the civil-unions registry. The law applies only when both spouses have no religion and thus is rarely used. According to the Justice Minister, only seventy-two couples registered under it in 2012–2014.

117 HCJ 143/62 Funk Schlesinger v. Minister of the Interior, P. D. 225 (1963), at http://versa.cardozo.yu.edu/opinions/funk-schlesinger-v-minister-interior.

Another development in the recognition of civil marriage abroad was Samuel v. Samuel,[118] in which the Supreme Court ruled that a woman married under civil auspices is entitled to alimony. The court reached this conclusion by combining civil and religious law and holding that because a woman married in a civil ceremony is held to be married under international law, she has the right to the alimony specified by religious law.

Private Marriage

Another method the court has recognized as a way to bypass the religious restrictions is marriage by private contract or in a private ceremony, without prior registration with the rabbinate.[119] According to halakhah, although a "kohen" (a member of the priestly families) may not ab initio wed a convert, a divorcee, or a "halutzah" (a widow exempted from the obligation of levirate marriage), such a marriage is valid post factum. The rabbinical courts are unwilling to recognize them, however, inasmuch as in this case halakhah requires the man to divorce his wife. Here the High Court ruled that the couple could have a religious ceremony in Israel, valid from a halakhic perspective, and the Interior Ministry must recognize their marriage as valid. Despite allowing such arrangements for a couple barred from marriage under halakhah, the Supreme Court did not open the door for this option in cases where the couple could have an official religious wedding. Doing so would have effectively left the Rabbinical Courts Law a dead letter.

These court decisions detracted from the religious courts' sole authority with regard to marriage in Israel and control over the definition of marriage. They created a situation in which Israeli Jews can marry abroad—even without setting foot outside of Israel if a foreign country provides what is effectively a mail order marriage certificate (so-called Paraguayan marriage). In 2000, then-Interior Minister Natan Sharansky proposed adding the option of "consular marriage"—a wedding held in the consulate of a foreign country, which again would eliminate the need to go abroad. The idea was prompted by the problem of the many immigrants from the former Soviet Union who are not recognized as Jews by halakhah and are not members of some other religious community.

---

118 Civil Appeal 566/81, Samuel v. Samuel, P. D. 39 (4) 309 (1985).

119 The High Court recognized private marriage in HCJ 130/66, Segev v. Rabbinical Court, P. D. 21 (2) 505 (1967).

Such a step would have effectively introduced civil marriage in Israel, but pressure by the religious parties kept it from being implemented.[120]

Recently, due to the growing popularity of private marriages that comply with the requirements of halakhah but are not conducted by the official rabbinate (including by couples who are halakhically ineligible to marry; see further below), the Marriage and Divorce (Registration) Ordinance was amended in 2013.[121] Under the amendment, those who marry or divorce outside the rabbinate or its authority are liable to a prison term of up to two years. As far as I know, this provision has never been enforced, but its presence in the law book reflects the increasing concern among the Orthodox officials about the loss of the chief rabbinate's monopoly on marriage (and divorce).

The initial recognition of common-law marriage came from the Knesset, after which the courts followed suit. The first step was an amendment to the Families of Fallen Soldiers (Pensions and Rehabilitation) Law 5710-1950. Its definition of "wife" included a woman who shared a household with a man and was publicly acknowledged as his spouse. A similar definition was added to other laws, including the Civil Service (Retirement) Law (Consolidated Version), 5730-1970; the Persons Disabled in the War against the Nazis Law 5714-1954; and Article 55 of the Inheritance Law 5725-1965, which recognizes the rights of the surviving spouse of a couple who live together as man and wife.

The Supreme Court, too, anchored the rights of common-law spouses and extended them even beyond what the legislature had provided. For example, in the Fessler case the Supreme Court ruled that a common-law wife can be deemed a married woman.[122] This ruling strikes a radical blow at halakhah, in that it legitimizes a quasi-marital relationship for a woman who has not been divorced from her husband and grants her the full rights of a wife—when for halakhah she is simply an adulterer.[123] This makes divorce less essential. In practice, however, the ruling did not lead to many such cases, because any children born to the woman in such a relationship are "mamzerim"—halakhically illegitimate—that is, among those ineligible for marriage under religious law.

---

120 Arie Dayan, "No Consulate Weddings and Italian Option is Out," *Ha'aretz*, May 15, 2003.

121 Passed by the Knesset on Oct. 28, 2013. The bill and explanatory notes were published in *Knesset Bills* 453, March 19, 2012, 145.

122 Civil Appeal 384/61, State of Israel v. Fessler, P. D. 16 102 (1962).

123 The basic concern is children born to the woman may be deemed *mamzerim* (halakhically illegitimate). On the halakhic status of a common-law wife, see Eliav Shochatman, "Is There a Possible Question of Kiddushin [Binding Betrothal] in a Common-Law Relationship?" *Meḥkerei Mishpat* 10 (5753): 7. [Heb.].

In addition to recognizing the possibility of couples in which the woman has not obtained a divorce from her husband, the court also recognized the validity of alimony payments to a common-law wife.[124] Later, in the early 1980s, the court also ruled that the presumption of community property between spouses also applies to common-law couples.[125] Both of these rulings, like Fessler, reduced the jurisdiction of the religious courts, since they grant a common-law wife the de jure status of every other wife (and effectively recognize such a couple as married),[126] but the jurisdiction over such a couple with regard to the division of property and child custody falls to the civil courts rather than the religious courts.

Change from Below

Israelis' willingness to have an Orthodox ceremony under the auspices of the official rabbinate has diminished over the years. Surveys show that half of Jewish Israelis, including most of those who identify as secular, would prefer not to marry through the rabbinate and not to be subject to the rabbinical courts in order to terminate their bond—if such an alternative existed.[127] Today there are several organizations that assist couples who wish to formalize their relationship without the involvement of the official rabbinate[128]—whether this means by a non-Orthodox rabbi (Masorti [Conservative] or Progressive [Reform]),[129] or by a totally secular organization. In the absence of civil marriage, these couples are common-law spouses.

In addition to the heterodox movements, several organizations offer these couples procedural and ritual support services.[130] One of them formulated

---

124 Civil Appeal 563/65, Jaeger (Flink) v. Palevitz, P. D. (3) 224 (1966).

125 Civil Appeal 52/80. Shachar v. Friedman, P. D. 38 (1) 443 (1984).

126 See Shachar Lifshitz, *Cohabitation Law in Israel: in Light of a Civil Law Theory of the Family* (Haifa: University of Haifa Press, 2005), 23 [Heb.]; Aharon Barak, "The Constitution of the Family: Constitutional Aspects of Family Law," *Mishpat ve-Asakim* 16 (2013): 13, 41 [Heb.].

127 According to the *Religion and State Index* published by the Hiddush organization in September 2017, 50% of the Jewish citizens of Israel would prefer to marry outside the rabbinate, and 84% of the nonreligious would prefer to do so (see Kobi Nahshoni, "Religion and State Index: The Jews in Israel are Less Religious," Ynet, Sept. 18, 2017).

128 A prominent player in this domain is Tzohar, which was authorized to register marriages as an alternative to the chief rabbinate by the Law to Amend the Marriage Ordinance (Registration) (Registration Areas) 5770-2009.

129 For example, Ceremonies and Conversions—Weddings, a major site for advanced Judaism; About a Traditional Wedding, the traditionalist movement website, https://www.beit-daniel.org.il/ceremonies/weddings/.

130 For example, "Wedding Ceremonies," Havaya, https://www.havaya.info/weddings/.

a "couplehood certificate," which it issues to those who wish to cement their relationship with a financial agreement.[131] This certificate has received implicit recognition in case law.[132] These organizations report that many couples have chosen to utilize their services and not marry through the chief rabbinate. In addition to the secular and non-Orthodox channels, in recent years there has been Orthodox competition with the chief rabbinate. The weddings project launched by Tzohar, an organization of liberal Orthodox rabbis, which eased some of the obstacles to registering for a marriage license, eventually gained official recognition and even specific legislation permitting it.[133] Although this scheme partially undermines the chief rabbinate's monopoly, the latter does recognize such marriages. A more serious threat to the chief rabbinate is posed by Orthodox rabbis who conduct ceremonies for couples who have not registered with the chief rabbinate. There is no doubt as to the halakhic validity of these ceremonies. But the threat they pose to the chief rabbinate was perceived as so great that in 2013 the Knesset made such a ceremony a criminal offense for the officiant and couple.[134]

The Civil Union for Citizens with No Religious Affiliation Law 5771-2010[135] allows two persons who do not belong to any of the recognized religious communities in Israel to register in the civil unions register and formalize their status as a family. This option does not erode the Status Quo, though, because until then such persons had not been able to marry at all. Because the law applies only when both spouses have no religion, it is rarely used: from its enactment until the beginning of 2018, only 127 couples took advantage of the law,[136] compared with the hundreds of thousands of couples who married in Israel during this period.

The options for attaining a status that resembles marriage and the recognition of civil marriages conducted abroad has led to a progressive increase in the number of those who choose to marry outside the rabbinate.

---

131 See the New Family Organization website: https://www.newfamily.org.il/.

132 See, "Selected Judgments by Judge Ayelet Golan Tavori" regarding Family case 11257-12-11, Anonymous v. Anonymous, Dec. 15, 2014.

133 This, too, by amending the Marriage and Divorce Ordinance (registration) (*supra* note 128).

134 Article 7 of the amendment to the Marriage and Divorce Ordinance (Registration) provides that "anyone who does not register his or her marriage or divorce, or the marriage or divorce he arranged for another party, is liable to two years' imprisonment." In other words, the rabbi who conducts the wedding or arranges the divorce faces criminal sanctions, and not only the couple, as previously. See Yair Ettinger, "A Wedding that Bypasses the Rabbinate," *Ha'aretz*, Oct. 21, 2011.

135 Civil Union for Citizens with No Religious Affiliation Law 5771-2010.

136 Reply to a freedom of information request by Meital Katz, supervisor of Freedom of Information in the Justice Ministry, dated Feb. 13, 2018.

According to the Central Bureau of Statistics, about 20% of the Israeli Jews who registered as married in 2013 had had a civil ceremony abroad;[137] the figure for 2017 was similar.[138] In addition to those who prefer to marry abroad and thereby be eligible for official recognition of their status, many employ some form of nonrecognized procedure inside Israel and forgo an official seal of marriage. Despite the chief rabbinate's attempt to curtail this phenomenon, it seems to be gaining momentum. Some believe that about a third of Israeli Jewish couples now choose to wed without benefit of the official clergy.[139]

The Erosion of the Status Quo on Divorce

The Religious Courts' Diminishing Jurisdiction

The Rabbinical Court Jurisdiction (Marriage and Divorce) Law 5713-1953 stipulates that halakhah will govern the marriage and divorce of Jews in Israel, and thus effectively grants the religious courts jurisdiction over divorce cases.[140] It is clear that in his Knesset speech about the importance of this law for the Jewish State of Israel, Warhaftig's focus was not on marriage but on divorce. This is because a couple who contract a halakhically valid marriage but then separate without a halakhic bill of divorce (even if they obtain a civil divorce)

---

137 This is an approximation of the true figure, since CBS data do not distinguish between Jews and non-Jews who married abroad and applied to have their marriage recognized in Israel. In addition, the number of marriages contracted abroad during a long stay there, rather than because of a desire to marry outside of the rabbinate, is about 10% of all marriages abroad (see "Natural Movement: Marriage and Divorce," 2013–2014, CBS, December 19, 2017, https://www.cbs.gov.il/he/publications/Pages/2017/%D7%AA%D7%A0%D7%95%D7%A2%D7%94-%D7%98%D7%91%D7%A2%D7%99%D7%AA-%D7%A0%D7%99%D7%A9%D7%95%D7%90%D7%99%D7%9F-%D7%95%D7%92%D7%99%D7%A8%D7%95%D7%A9%D7%99%D7%9F-2014-2013-.aspx).

138 This is evident from the CBS data; see "Data for Tu B'Av 2017," CBS, August 6, 2017, https://www.cbs.gov.il/he/mediarelease/Pages/2017/%D7%9C%D7%A7%D7%98-%D7%A0%D7%AA%D7%95%D7%A0%D7%99%D7%9D-%D7%9C%D7%A8%D7%92%D7%9C-%D7%98%D7%95-%D7%91%D7%90%D7%91-%D7%AA%D7%A9%D7%A2%D7%96-2017.aspx.

139 Tomer Persico, "Conversation with Rabbi David Stav," Tom Persico Website https://tomerpersico.com/2013/02/04/rav_stav_talk/. In the summer of 2014, Channel 10 broadcast a series of articles about the chief rabbinate's monopoly on marriage and divorce in Israel and its various implications.

140 For the essentials of divorce law in Judaism, see Lifshitz (*supra* note 126), 508–512.

are considered to be still married.[141] The repercussions of this situation for the woman's subsequent offspring are enormous. They are considered to be mamzerim whose halakhic marriage options are severely limited and who pass on the stigma to all their descendants. Should many such persons live in a community, there would be a need for genealogical records to prove that brides and grooms are free of this taint and the people could be split asunder.

The religious courts' monopoly on divorce, including the division of property and child custody, spawned great friction between halakhic norms and modern concepts of human rights and gender equality. The religious courts are criticized especially for dividing the couple's assets in accordance with halakhah (see below) and for applying the concept of divorce that stems. This requires that there be some "blemish" in one spouse, unlike the prevalent norm of no-fault divorce in the Western world today. Another problem is the abyss between rabbinical judges' worldview and that of most of the litigants who appear before them, who do not accept the legal principles, derived from religious belief, that are applied to their case.[142]

Common-Law Marriage

As we have seen above, the legal recognition of common law marriage by the courts and the legislature and the conferring of all the rights of a lawfully wedded wife on the woman effectively circumvents the need for a halakhic divorce. This path does not seem to have gained wide traction, however, because of the problems it raises, as well as the couple's natural desire for official recognition of their bond.

Division of Community Property

The unequal division of property following a divorce, as often prescribed by halakhah, is incompatible with the fundamental liberal principle of parity

141 With regard to the status of those who did not have a recognized religious wedding ceremony (those who had a civil ceremony or common-law spouses), there is a halakhic controversy, Some rabbis hold that such a couple still requires a religious divorce. See Rabbi Shlomo Dichovsky, "Civil Marriage," *Tehumin* 2 (5741): 252; Rabbi She'ar Yashuv Cohen, "Civil Marriage," *Tehumin* 3 (5742): 154. Others disagree (Dichovsky, "Civil Marriage").

142 Indeed, the High Court has been pushing the rabbinical courts to adapt their rulings to the standards and norms of Israeli law. See, for example, HCJ 3914/92, Lev. v. The Tel Aviv-Jaffa Regional Rabbinical Court, P. D. 48(2) 491 (1994).

between the spouses. Acutely aware of this problem, the Knesset and the Supreme Court have progressively reduced the status of religious law on the matter, to the point where religious courts have been stripped of the authority to follow the (religious) law they are supposed to implement.

A long series of enactments govern the award of alimony and child support and the division of property between the divorcing spouses, and assign the civil courts extensive power in these matters.[143]

Another significant step in this regard was the Bavli case, in which the Supreme Court intervened blatantly to effectively bind the rabbis' hands.[144] The ruling required them to apply the presumption of community property, the Marital Community Property Law 5733-1973, and the equitable mechanism enshrined in the law for the distribution of community property. In his decision, Justice Barak clearly spoke the language of rights, and in its name modified the Status Quo autonomy granted the rabbinical courts and required them to adhere to Israeli civil legislation:

> Universal civil law gives expression to basic human rights. . . .
>
> It is inconsistent with these fundamental concepts for the transfer [of a case] from a civil court to a religious court to result in the loss or infringement of these basic rights. We must not permit these civil rights to be "confiscated" without an express provision in law that satisfies the requirements set by our constitutional structure.[145]

In the years that passed since the Bavli case, many additional court rulings have violated the halakhic principles for the division of property between spouses.[146] Nevertheless, the rabbinical courts do not always honor them and sometimes still decree an unequal distribution of community property. They do so both by intentionally disregarding the Supreme Court's ruling and by invoking other legal mechanisms that alter the division of the couple's assets, usually to the woman's detriment. One of these mechanisms is the practice to require the return of gifts exchanged between husband and wife during their

143 For more on this, see Pinchas Shiffman, "Rabbinical Courts—Where?" *Mishpat u-mimshal* 2, no. 2 (5755): 523 [Heb.].

144 HCJ 1000/92, Bavli v. The Supreme Rabbinical Court of Jerusalem, P. D. 8(2) 221(1994).

145 Ibid., 248.

146 Including recent rulings, such as Family Appeal Request 919/15, Anonymous v. Anonymous (Dec. 6, 2016, not yet published), in which the court deviated from Jewish law and held that the woman's income should be taken into account in a case of joint child custody.

marriage. On the surface this is fair and equal and operates in both directions, but in practice its implementation usually discriminates against the woman.

The Husband's Refusal to Grant a Divorce

Under halakhah, a woman cannot divorce her husband. The man must voluntarily convey the physical bill of divorce—the *get*—to her. The problem of "*get* refusal," when he will not do so, is at the top of the list of the problems created by the halakhah with regard to personal status, in terms both of the number of cases[147] and the religious court's difficulty in resolving it. It leads to harsh criticism of the religious court system and its judges and has served as a major catalyst for erosion of the Status Quo in marriage and divorce. To date, however, the Supreme Court has not intervened in such cases and has not arrogated the right to declare a couple divorced when the rabbinical courts will not. The root of the problem is the halakhic conception of marriage and consequently of the procedure for ending it and dissolving the relationship. Under most Western legal codes (continuing the Christian Protestant tradition), in certain circumstances a court may decree a divorce without the consent of both parties. In Jewish law, by contrast, divorce requires specific action by both the man and the woman—the husband's physical conveyance of the *get* to the wife and her acceptance of the document.[148] More importantly, the conveyance must be voluntary on both sides in order to be valid. The procedure is invalid if the husband granted the divorce as a result of external coercion.[149]

Nevertheless, in some situations halakhah permits the religious court to intervene and grant a divorce against the will of one of the parties. When there are halakhic grounds to terminate the marriage, the court can compel the husband or wife to grant or accept the divorce. The causes mentioned in the Talmud are limited and apply mainly to the woman (such as illness and physical

---

147 There is no clear information about how many women are refused a divorce. According to the rabbinical courts, no more than a few hundred such cases are pending. The women's organizations put the figure at 13,000–15,000. This large disparity stems from fundamentally different definitions of divorce refusal. See Yaron Unger and Orly Almagor Lotan, *Divorce Refusal in Israel: The Halakhic and Legal Background, the Scope of the Phenomenon, and Methods for Dealing with It*, Knesset Research and Information Center, March 13, 2011, 13–17 [Heb.].

148 For the fundamentals of divorce laws in Judaism, see Lifshitz (*supra* note 126), 508–512.

149 Accordingly, if the woman enters into a relationship with another man after such a "coerced divorce," the relationship is adulterous and any children born to the couple will be halakhically illegitimate.

defects).[150] Later, the grounds were expanded to include misconduct by the husband or wife, with the further stipulation that in such cases the court could compel the guilty party to grant or accept the divorce. The Talmudic form of coercion—lashing the recalcitrant spouse until he says "I want to give it"[151]—would be illegal in Israel today. However, the Rabbinical Courts (Marriage and Divorce) Law 5713-1953 does envisage the possibility of an involuntary divorce; the Rabbinic Courts Law (Enforcement of Divorce Rulings) 5755-1995 adds various sanctions against noncompliant spouses, including the possibility of imprisonment of a man who refuses to obey the court's ruling that he divorce his wife.[152] This is a case where external social pressure to resolve the problem of divorce refusal, with the severe infringement of the victim's rights, prompted the Knesset to provide the religious courts with tools, compatible with halakhah, to "encourage" the spouse to want a divorce. Were it up to the rabbinical court judges, however, some would probably not employ these measures and do so only due to the strong public pressure.[153]

Change from Below

Divorce is the one area where the rabbinical courts' monopoly remains nearly untouched—but some cracks have begun to appear. Under halakhah, any panel of three observant men (even if they lack rabbinic judicial qualification) can set themselves up as a tribunal and issue halakhically binding decisions. Over

---

150 In the time of the Mishnah, the matter was not as serious, since only the husband's consent was required for a divorce.

151 Because the fundamental requirement of divorce law is that both parties consent, a technique was halakhically constructed to "force him until he says I want." That is, the tribunal may exert physical sanction (lashes) on the husband until he expresses his desire to divorce. The understanding is that in such a case, physical coercion reveals the will of the coerced, and therefore the act of giving the divorce is by will. Therefore, even in the case of coercion of divorce, it is not the act of the tribunal that creates the divorce, as is the case with other legal methods, but in the action of the tribunal that brings the parties into a state of will, so that eventually the divorce is done by the will of both parties.

152 One of the allegations made is that the rabbinical courts have not made adequate use of the sanctions provided by Israeli law to enforce their divorce orders. Whether "adequate" or not, they have indeed avoided the massive use of the methods stipulated in the Rabbinical Court Laws (Divorce Judgments) 1995 and its amendments, for fear that such a divorce would be "coerced" and thus invalid.

153 In her book, Rivka Lubitsch describes the tribulations of women in the rabbinical courts and shows that the judges are loath to invoke such sanctions (*From the End of the World to the End: The Torment of Women in the Rabbinical Court* [Rishon Lezion: Miskal, 2017] [Heb.].

the years, in fact, private religious courts in the ultraorthodox sector, with no recognition by the state, have issued divorce decrees. Such panels are also employed by couples who are not members of the ultraorthodox community but for various reasons prefer to marry and divorce through them. Because these courts operate discreetly, there are no data on the number of couples divorced through them. Today, with the mounting public distrust of the official rabbinical court system,[154] rabbis who are not ultraorthodox have cautiously begun convening private courts to grant divorces when the courts of the official rabbinate cannot or decline to do so.[155]

Summary

When it comes to marriage and divorce, the erosion of the Status Quo and changes in the arrangements that prevailed under the Mandate and were consolidated in the early years of statehood are clear and unmistakable.[156] The rise of liberal values and the willingness to give less weight to or abandon traditional values that conflict with modern ideas has produced real change on this issue. Supreme court rulings over the years have reduced the religious courts' authority and jurisdiction as conferred by the Rabbinical Courts Law (Marriage and Divorce) Law 5713-1953. The Supreme Court has found various ways to get around the law's stipulation that marriage in Israel be conducted according to Torah law and has permitted a broad range of marriage and partnership arrangements that have nothing to do with the rabbinical system. Today, although the rabbinical

---

154 Recently, after a state rabbinical court found no remedy for a woman who had been refused a divorce for many years, three Orthodox rabbis set up a private court and annulled the marriage. This technique, though very different than divorce, has the same result: the woman is no longer considered married. See Eliav Shochatman, "Annulling Kiddushin: A Possible Way to Solve the Problem of those Denied a Divorce?" *Hebrew Law Annual* (5767/1999): 349. According to one of the judges on that court, they would not hesitate to arrange a divorce if deemed necessary.

155 See "Private Religious Court Annuls the Marriage of a Woman Whose Husband Fled to the United States," Hiddush, Sept. 8, 2013 https://www.hiddush.org.il/%D7%9E%D7%90%D7%9E%D7%A8-4251-0-%D7%91%D7%99%D7%AA_%D7%93%D7%99%D7%9F_%D7%A4%D7%A8%D7%98%D7%99_%D7%91%D7%99%D7%98%D7%9C_%D7%A0%D7%99%D7%A9%D7%95%D7%90%D7%99_%D7%90%D7%A9%D7%94_%D7%A9%D7%91%D7%A2%D7%9C%D7%94_%D7%A0%D7%9E%D7%9C%D7%98_%D7%9C%D7%90%D7%A8%D7%94%D7%91.aspx. See also Yair Ettinger, "Divorcing the Rabbinate," *Ha'aretz*, Oct. 28, 2011.

156 Unlike the issue of the Sabbath, where many of the arrangements depend on conventions, making it difficult to accurately measure the impact of liberalization of Israeli democracy and society.

system no longer has exclusivity in this area, there is still no formal alternative of civil marriage, as found in the rest of the world. Marriages or partnerships that do result from a legally recognized religious marriage depend on a set of patchwork and not always coherent solutions.

The changes in the religious courts' jurisdiction over divorce are due mainly to Supreme Court rulings but are also rooted in Knesset legislation. Those who formulated the Status Quo and drafted legislation enshrining it envisaged a country in which personal status laws were regulated in strict accordance with halakhah. But the ascendancy of liberal values and the general unwillingness of the legislature and courts to affirm religious law when it contradicts those values have led to the eclipse of this vision.

Here, too, the change has been led from below, by civil society organizations and the general public. More and more couples are "voting with their rings" and turning their back on the official system of religious services—even those who could marry through it.[157] If this trend grows, the quantity can turn into quality and affect the Status Quo even further, to the point that the rabbinic monopoly ceases to exist.

2.3 Who Is a Jew and Who Is a Convert?

Introduction

The issue of who is Jewish and what constitutes a valid conversion to Judaism is a major issue in the fabric of religious and state relations in Israel.[158] As mentioned, the definition of who is a Jew did not receive explicit attention in the original Status Quo, because there was no need to address it then. The Law of Return, 5710-1950, was enacted two years after independence and until 1958 the issue did not provoke significant public debate.[159] Since then, however, the issue has remained in the public consciousness. From 1958 to 1970, when the

---

157 This trend is also reflected in surveys that show that many of the secular and a considerable number of the religious would like there to be alternatives to marriage through the rabbinate.

158 The issue also has dramatic implications for the relations between the State of Israel and Diaspora Jewry. See Theodore Sasson, Benjamin Phillips, Charles Kadushin, and Leonard Saxe, *Still Connected: American Jewish Attitudes About Israel* (Waltham: Brandeis University, Maurice and Marilyn Cohen Center for Modern Jewish Studies, 2010). For more information on conversion, see Nathaniel Fisher, *The Conversion Challenge in Israel: Policy Analysis and Recommendations*, Policy Study 103 (Jerusalem: The Israeli Democracy Institute, 2015).

159 See Warhaftig's comments on this understanding of the conversion process (Warhaftig, *Constitution*, 551).

Law of Return was amended to clarify the matter, the question was: "Who is a Jew?" Since then, the burning issue has been what conversions are valid and recognized in Israel.

Here too, the Status Quo that granted the chief rabbinate a de facto monopoly on valid conversions in Israel has eroded, due to the courts' recognition of non-Orthodox conversions and of Orthodox conversions performed by private rabbinic tribunals without the chief rabbinate's involvement. Recently there has been a "bottom up" push, in the form of private Orthodox conversions by a network of tribunals, Giyur K'Halacha, which challenges the exclusivity of the chief rabbinate in the Orthodox world. The most recent chapter in this saga is a report written by Moshe Nissim (a former justice minister and the son of the Sephardi chief rabbi in the 1950s) at the request of the prime minister, which suggested the establishment of a conversion authority that would be independent of the chief rabbinate.[160]

The original text of the Law of Return, enacted in 1950, states simply that "every Jew is entitled to immigrate to Israel."[161] The 1970 amendment[162] defines a Jew as "a person born to a Jewish mother or someone who converted and does not belong to a different religion."[163] This amendment raises several issues: (1) Through a liberal-critical prism, the Law of Return, which is practically the citizenship law of the State of Israel,[164] discriminates against non-Jews and contradicts basic values of equality.[165] (2) In the narrower aspect too, there is a wide range of possible interpretations of who is a Jew and what constitutes a valid conversion—from the Orthodox interpretation based strictly on halakhah to a

---

160 Although Nissim recommended that the Orthodox establishment be given a monopoly on conversion in Israel, his proposal is unlikely to pass the Knesset because of the opposition of the ultraorthodox parties. For the full document, see Moshe Nissim, "The Conversion in Israel: Report and Recommendations," Jerusalem, 2018 (shorturl.at/cwxRW(. https://www.srugim.co.il/wp-content/uploads/2018/06/%D7%94%D7%92%D7%99%D7%95%D7%A8-%D7%91%D7%99%D7%A9%D7%A8%D7%90%D7%9C-%D7%93%D7%95%D7%97-%D7%95%D7%94%D7%9E%D7%9C%D7%A6%D7%95%D7%AA-2018-1.pdf.

161 The Law of Return was passed by the Knesset on July 5, 1950.

162 Adopted by the Knesset on March 10, 1970.

163 The Law of Return, 1950, section 4b (Law Book 5760, No. 586, March 19, 1970, Bill 5730, 34; Law 866, 36, Amendment No. 2).

164 The Israeli citizenship law (1952) provides a procedure for naturalization, but the vast majority of immigrants Israel are entitled to citizenship under the Law of Return or by marriage to Israelis.

165 On the dilemma faced by Israel as a liberal democracy that is also a nation-state, see Yoav Peled, "Will the State of Israel Be the State of All Its Citizens in Its Centenary Year?" in *The Law in Israel: Looking to the Future*, ed. Yedidia Z. Stern, Yaffa Zilbershatz, and Itai Lipshitz (Ramat Gan: Bar-Ilan University, 2003), 239 [Heb.].

pluralistic concept based on broad national definitions of conversion and not bound by religious norms. The adherence by the state or one of its institutions (the chief rabbinate) to a particular interpretation may deny the right of return to those whom that institution does not recognize as Jews. (3) This situation may also violate the right to marry of those whom the chief rabbinate does not recognize as Jews.[166]

Who Is a Jew?

Before the Amendment of the Law of Return

Until 1958, the legal definition, derived from the Mandatory Religious Community (Conversion) Ordinance[167] and the practice in effect after independence, was that a Jew is a person defined as such by halakhah.[168] That year, Interior Minister Israel Bar-Yehuda of the leftist Ahdut Ha'avoda party instructed the population registrar that anyone who declared in good faith that he was a Jew would be registered as such, and that if parents declared their child Jewish the child would be registered as such, even if the mother was not Jewish.[169] The new regulations triggered a severe coalition crisis and were eventually modified about two years later, when Haim Moshe Shapiro of the National Religious Party became interior minister.[170]

---

166 At the far end of the discussion of Jewish identity is the concept of Jewish self-determination, prevalent in the United States but hardly relevant in Israel; see Shlomo Fisher and Susan Last Stone, *Jewish Identity and Identification: New Patterns, Meanings, and Networks* (Jerusalem: Jewish People Policy Institute, 2012). In a certain sense, but different from the modern one, the Shalit affair (*supra* note 8; *infra*, note 331) represents the concept of Judaism by self-definition, accepted for entry in the population registry, under the specific circumstances of the affair.

167 Article 1 of this 1927 Mandatory ordinance, which is still in effect, states that in order for a religious conversion to have legal force the convert must submit confirmation of the change of status from the head of the religious congregation that he or she wishes to join. For Jews, this is the chief rabbi of Israel.

168 Warhaftig, *Constitution*, 155; Don-Yehiya (Ibid., 32, note 51), 88, 91.

169 Bar-Yehuda's guidelines were based on the opinion of then-Attorney General Haim Cohen, who stated that "there is no escape from the fact that the existing outcome and the religious decision is different in its content and nature from the secular decision-making process. The fact that a person is considered a non-Jew according to the religion of Moses and Israel does not prevent and does not contradict that this person may be so considered for the purposes of implementing laws that apply to a Jew, and vice versa"(Warhaftig, *Constitution*, 156).

170 This crisis led to the establishment of a government committee to resolve it. It also led Ben-Gurion to write a letter to "the sages of Israel," Orthodox and non-Orthodox intellectuals, asking them to express their answer to the question of who is considered a Jew. Most of them (thirty-five of forty-five who responded) opted for some version of the Orthodox concept.

The next crises on this front were the Rufeisen and Shalit cases. In 1962, Rev. Samuel Oswald Rufeisen (better known as "Brother Daniel") asked the High Court to order the population registrar to recognize him as a Jew under the Law of Return.[171] Rufeisen was born and raised a Jew; but during the Holocaust he took refuge in a convent and was baptized. Later he joined the Carmelite Order. In 1958 he arrived in Israel and sought to be recognized as a Jew under the Law of Return. The Interior Ministry declined to do so and he appealed to the High Court, which ruled four to one against him.[172] It held that, although most interpretations of halakhah deemed him to still be a Jew, the Law of Return, which is a "secular law," is not bound by this.[173]

The next significant development came in 1970, in the Shalit case.[174] Benjamin Shalit was an Israeli naval officer married to a non-Jew, who sought to have his children (not Jewish under halakhah) registered as Jews by nationality. In its five to four ruling, the Supreme Court ruled in his favor, deciding that the government could not base its decision about nationality on halakhah. In these two cases the court adopted a national definition of Judaism and rejected the halakhic religious definition. Political turmoil ensued.

The Amendment of the Law of Return and the Question of a Valid Conversion

In reaction to the Shalit ruling, the Knesset amended the Law of Return by adding section 4B, which states that "for the purposes of this law, a Jew is defined as a person born to a Jewish mother or one who converted, and does not belong to a different religion." However, because the stipulation is not "converted

---

See "Exchange of Letters between Prime Minister David Ben-Gurion and Israeli Sages on the Question of Who Is a Jew," Israel State Archives, PMO-GovernmentSecretary-000sces. This file includes the initial letter, the list of respondents, and their answers. The letters were also collected by Eliezer Ben-Raphael in *Jewish Identities: Answers of the Sages of Israel to Ben-Gurion* (Sde Boker: Ben-Gurion Heritage Center and Ben-Gurion University of the Negev, 2001) [Heb.].

171 HCJ 72/62, Rufeisen v. Minister of the Interior, P. D. 16, 2428 (1962).

172 Justice Haim Cohen reiterated the opinion he had expressed when serving as attorney general and supported the regulations published by Interior Minister Bar-Yehuda.

173 The court extensively analyzed the halakhic positions on this issue and held that according to Jewish law a converted Jew is a Jew. This position is not accepted by all decisors. See, for example, Aharon Lichtenstein, *Musar Aviv: On Morality, Faith and Society* (Jerusalem and Alon Shvut: Maggid and Yeshivat Har Etzion, 259) [Heb.]. Rabbi Lichtenstein holds that an apostate like Brother Daniel, who converted to Christianity and took holy orders, is such an extreme case that it is doubtful he can be considered a Jew.

174 The Shalit affair (*supra* note 8).

according to the Jewish law" but merely "converted," the amendment opened a whole new can of worms: What is a valid conversion for the purposes of to the Law of Return and the population registry?[175] There followed repeated attempts to fill this lacuna and legislate that a Jew is a person converted according to halakhah.[176]

Today the core of this battle is the recognition of non-Orthodox conversions. Not only does this issue divide the Israeli public in Israel, it creates a serious conflict between the State of Israel and Diaspora Jewry, especially in the United States.

The Erosion of the Status Quo on Conversion through Court Rulings

After the passage of the amendment, only those converted under Orthodox auspices were registered as Jews.[177] The validity of non-Orthodox conversions first came before the Supreme Court in the case of Shoshana (Susan) Miller, who had had a Reform conversion in the United States.[178] At first the interior minister refused to register her as a Jew. Then, when he realized that he could not avoid doing so, he announced that the annotation "(converted)" would be appended to the word "Jewish" on her identity card. In response to Miller's petition, the court ruled that under the Population Registry Law, nationality and religion must be registered only on the basis of the applicant's notification, and that the registrar does not have the authority to add details as he sees fit (such as "converted"). In other words, a person who converted outside of Israel under non-Orthodox auspices must be seen as Jew for the Law of Return and the population registry.

---

175 Regarding the halakhic problem of this type of conversion and its recognition, see Rabbi Haim David Halevy, *Religion and State* (Tel Aviv: n.p., 5765), 49–65 [Heb.].

176 Starting with the political "reversal" of 1977 and for a decade after, the religious parties endeavored to amend the Law of Return and to state that a Jew is one who converted properly. Although Prime Minister Menachem Begin supported this, he, and later Yitzhak Shamir and Shimon Peres, did not push the change because of opposition by members of their own factions and other coalition parties, along with considerable opposition by the non-Orthodox, especially in the United States. Even some members of the religious parties in the Knesset did not give it their full support, because of the sensitivity of the issue. The other factor that pushed Knesset members to promote the amendment was the High Court rulings in the Miller and Shas Movement cases (see below). See Eliezer Don-Yehiya, "Who is a Jew, Who is a Convert? The Attempts to Amend Legislation and Their Failure," in *The Fourth Decade: 5738-5748*, ed. Yehiam Weitz and Zvi Zameret (Jerusalem: Yad Yitzhak Ben-Zvi, 2002) 69 [Heb.].

177 Until the High Court of Justice changed the situation (see below).

178 HCJ 230/86, Miller v. the Minister of the Interior, P. D. 436 (4) (1986).

Another ruling that goes in the same direction as Miller was handed down on a petition filed by the Sephardi Torah Association (Shas Movement).[179] Chief Justice Meir Shamgar ruled that if immigrants submit a document or certificate attesting to their conversion in a Jewish community abroad, the registrar must record them as Jewish. Any conversion must be recognized, whether under Orthodox, Conservative, or Reform auspices, even if the converts did not become an active member of the communities in which they converted.

These ruling spurred the religious parties to increasing efforts to legislate that only conversions according to halakhah would be recognized as valid. They were moved in part by their concerns about mass immigration to Israel and the inability to identify a Jew under halakhah on the basis of the nationality clause on his or her Israeli identity card. In an attempt to resolve the dispute about the registration of Jews converted abroad, a ministerial committee was set up; it heard all relevant parties but never issued a report. After the 1988 elections, another committee was formed, including representatives of the non-Orthodox streams abroad. It reached certain agreements but its recommendations were not implemented.[180]

The next stage of the struggle about "who is a convert" and the ongoing modification of the Status Quo (from the situation in the early years of the state) was the Pasero (Goldstein) decision.[181] In this case, the court dealt with recognition of non-Orthodox conversions completed in Israel. According to its ruling, interpretation of the Religious Communities (Conversion) Ordinance must take account of the principles of equality and of freedom of conscience and religion; hence it should be interpreted narrowly so that it does not exclude recognition of non-Orthodox conversion in Israel for the purpose of registration. But the court did not take the next steps and did not recognize non-Orthodox conversions conducted in Israel as grounds for registration as a Jew and eligibility to make aliya under the Law of Return.

The Pasero (Goldstein) case influenced the coalition agreement between the Likud and the religious parties after the 1996 elections, which included a promise to prevent recognition of non-Orthodox conversions in Israel. The government approved a conversion to guarantee this, which passed its first reading in the Knesset. This triggered fierce protests by the Reform and Conservative movements, in Israel and abroad, and a campaign to prevent its

---

179 HCJ 264/87, Sephardi Torah Association—Shas Movement v. Director of Population Registration Administration, P. D. 43 (2) 730 (1989).

180 Elyakim Rubinstein, *Paths of Government and Law: Public Law Issues in Israel* (Tel Aviv: MOD, 2003), 208 [Heb.].

181 HCJ 1031/93, Pasero (Goldstein) v. Minister of the Interior, PD 49(4) 661 (1995).

passage. Representatives of the movements in North America went so far as to threaten to halt their financial contributions to Israel and to sever ties with the country.[182]

In 1995, the chief rabbinate established a state conversion system, which later became the base for the system of conversion courts.[183] The system, which has undergone various administrative metamorphoses and been shunted from one ministry to another, remains the backbone of the state conversion system today.[184] Although this step was supposed to make Orthodox conversions more accessible, many believe that it has had the opposite result.

In the wake of the Supreme Court rulings on conversion, in 1997 the government established a committee, headed by Prof. Yaakov Neeman (former minister of justice and finance). After hearing all concerned parties and discussing the matter, the committee proposed the establishment of a joint conversion institute with representatives from all streams of Judaism, with the actual conversion at the end of the process following the Orthodox procedure. The Neeman Committee's recommendations were adopted in part and culminated in the establishment of a joint conversion preparation organization, Nativ,[185] leading to a full Orthodox conversion. Another conversion system that is also subject to the chief rabbinate's conversion system was established within the army. It allows non-Jewish soldiers to study for conversion and even to convert in a military setting.[186]

More fuel was added to the conversion dispute by the court's decision in two cases. In the Na'amat case,[187] it ruled that non-Orthodox conversions performed in Israel must be recognized as valid for the purpose of the nationality clause, meaning that the population registrar must list the convert as a Jew. In the Rodriguez Toshbeim case, the court ruled that a non-Orthodox conversion of an individual who studied for conversion in Israel and then went abroad for a short

---

182 See Shimon Sheetrit, *Between Three Authorities: The Balance of Civil Rights in Religious Affairs in Israel* (Jerusalem: Floersheimer Institute for Policy Studies, 1999), 20 [Heb.].

183 The procedures to be followed by the system came into effect only in 2006 (see "Rules of Procedure for Conversion Requests, 2006," Women's Justice Center, accessed 12 July 2022, https://www.cwj.org.il/orc/126).

184 See Yisrael Rosen, "15 Years of State Conversion from a Personal and Public Angle," Zomet Institute, accessed July 5, 2022, https://www.zomet.org.il/?CategoryID=281&ArticleID=650.

185 See Naomi Mei-Ami, *The Issue of Conversion in Israel*, Knesset Research and Information Center, June 25, 2007, 7 [Heb.].

186 See Amiram Barkat, "The IDF Leads Friendly Conversion, and Hundreds of Immigrants Convert Every Year," *Ha'aretz*, Nov. 22, 2005.

187 HCJ 5070/95, Na'amat—Working Women and Volunteers v. Minister of the Interior, PD 56(2) (721) (2002).

time to undergo the conversion ceremony in a Jewish community there must be recognized for the purpose of the Law of Return.[188] Nevertheless, Interior Minister Eli Yishai (who took office shortly after these decisions) announced that he would issue orders to implement the court decisions and that his and the other religious parties would endeavor to circumvent the court's ruling through legislation. Yishai even ordered that the nationality clause be deleted from Israeli identity cards so that he would not have to register non-Orthodox converts as Jews.[189]

The Internal Orthodox Struggle over Conversion and the Erosion of State Conversion: Change from Below

There have been several developments in the field of conversion in recent years. The most recent of them is the most significant, both with regard to conversion itself and in the context of the weakening the Status Quo overall.

The state and military conversion system was established by religious Zionists, who controlled it for many years. In 2008, ultraorthodox members of the Supreme Rabbinical Court objected to a policy they saw as too lenient. A panel headed by Rabbi Avraham Sherman issued two rulings that set a precedent and were controversial in both the halakhic and political realms. It held that all the conversions signed by Rabbi Haim Druckman, the long-time head of the conversion system, were null and void.[190] The Israeli Supreme Court criticized the decision but decided not to intervene.[191] Subsequently, then-Sephardi Chief Rabbi Shlomo Moshe Amar[192] initiated a change in procedure so that one court

---

188 HCJ 2859/99, Macrinaia v. Minister of the Interior, P. D. 59 (6) 721 (2004); HCJ 2597/99 Rodriguez-Toshbeim v. Minister of the Interior, P. D. 58 (5) 412 (2005).

189 See Anshel Pfeiffer, Gideon Alon, and Mazal Moalem, "The Nationality Clause Will Be Deleted from ID Cards," *Ha'aretz*, March 14, 2002.

190 Case 5489-64-1, Anonymous, Anonymous, and Anonymous (published in Nevo, 10.2.2008); and 6122-21-1, Anonymous v. Anonymous (published in Nevo, May 10, 2009). The court based its decision on procedural flaws that it deemed to have affected the proceedings. At the heart of the halakhic debate is the stringency of the requirement that the convert accept the duty to comply with the religious precepts. Those who are more stringent would check on the convert later; if he or she is found to be violating the commandments, there are grounds for annulling the conversion. The more lenient examine the convert's sincerity at the moment of conversion. An even more lenient approach is that the convert's intention is to join the people of Israel and there is no need for full observance of all the precepts.

191 HCJ 5079/08, Anonymous v. Dayan Rabbi Sherman (published in Nevo, April 25, 2012).

192 For Rabbi Amar's halakhic position on the annulment of a conversion, see Rabbi Haim Amsalem, *Cancellation of Conversion Due to Dishonesty of Acceptance of Mitzvot: Comments*

can no longer invalidate conversions performed by another court. In the end, the conversions were not nullified, but a heavy political and halakhic cloud enveloped on the conversion system. In an effort to demonstrate that it was blameless and show deference to the ultraorthodox position and avoid future disqualifications, the state conversion system adopted a more stringent policy.[193]

Private conversions by Orthodox rabbis are another significant development that originated from the ground up. In 2016, several major religious Zionist rabbis established their own unofficial conversion court. For rabbis to whom the integrity and authority of the rabbinate was insignificant when compared to their own (such as Rabbi David Stav, a modern-Orthodox rabbi, who stood as a candidate for chief rabbi), this indicated a lack of faith in the conversion system that operated under the auspices of the state and the chief rabbinate.[194] These rabbis effectively set up a parallel system of religious services; because those converted by these tribunals will not be recognized as Jews by the chief rabbinate, they will need to wed privately outside the rabbinate. Some of these rabbis involved in this conversion project have stated that they are willing to take this complementary step as well.[195]

The private Orthodox conversions soon achieved recognition, even if indirect, by the Supreme Court. Several individuals who were converted by the private court of an extreme ultraorthodox community in Jerusalem applied for recognition of their conversion. The Supreme Court held that the rabbinical court of a recognized and established religious community could perform conversions and that the state must recognize them. This shattered the chief rabbinate's monopoly over Orthodox conversion in Israel and opened the door to large-scale, halakhically valid conversions that would be recognized for registration as Jewish in the Population Registry.[196] The ruling led the ultraorthodox Knesset factions to submit a bill that would overturn it. It was in response to world Jewry's vigorous protests that Moshe Nissim was asked to draft recommendations on the issue.[197] He proposed some slight reforms in

---

by Knesset Member Rabbi Chaim Amsalem . . . (Jerusalem: self-published, 5765), 72 [Heb.].

193 See, for example, a position paper by Itim, "Conversion in Israel," submitted to the Knesset Committee for the Advancement of Women's Status and Gender Equality, June 9, 2014, 2 [Heb.].

194 See Yair Ettinger, "Senior Rabbis against the Rabbinate: Establish an Alternative Body to Conduct Mass Conversions," *Ha'aretz*, August 10, 2015; Giyur K'Halacha, https://www.giyur.org.il/.

195 Zvika Klein, "Much Grief: Rabbi Riskin's War on Justice," nrg, Aug. 5, 2017.

196 HCJ 7625/06, Rogachova v. the Interior Ministry (published in Nevo, March 31, 2016).

197 See Barak Ravid, "Netanyahu Appoints Former Justice Minister Moshe Nissim to Submit Recommendations on Conversion Issue," *Ha'aretz*, August 16, 2017.

the existing arrangement, centered on the establishment of a state conversion authority with representatives of all streams, but dominated by the Orthodox. He would continue to recognize non-Orthodox conversions performed abroad, but not in Israel, and allow city rabbis to serve as conversion judges in the assemblies in which the rule of the majority will determine the outcome of potential conversion.[198] The report was submitted to the prime minister in June 2018 but has been rejected by the ultraorthodox parties.[199]

The recognition in non-orthodox conversion in Israel: Due to the rejection of the Nissim recommendations, the High Court of Justice had to decide in the very long put off petition of the Reform and Conservative steams. In these petitions they demanded that the court will order the state to recognize the conversion they are commanding in Israel as a conversion that meets the requirement of the Law of Return that defines as Jewish someone that "converted." In its decision in the Dahan v. the Interior Minister case[200] that was given sixteen(!) years after it was submitted to the court, the court ruled that a non-Orthodox conversion would be officially recognized for the sake of the Law of Return. In its decision, the court lengthy described the government's efforts through the years to achieve an agreed solution and therefore to render the decision of the court unnecessary. In this case as well, the court described Israeli government nearly begging it to take a decision. The failure of politicians to so forced the court to decide. Based on its previous decisions to recognize non-Orthodox conversion abroad[201] and private Orthodox conversion in Israel, the court has finally also recognized non-Orthodox conversion in Israel. The decision was sharply criticized by Orthodox and right wing politicians, blaming the court for taking political decisions. But beside statements, they again failed to take any concrete measures to reverse it.

The Orthodox conversion reform: The last chapter in the "who is a convert" saga is the reform within the Orthodox conversion system that the Bennet government tried to promote. The Orthodox community in Israel are concerned that there are about 500,000 immigrants from the former Soviet-Union who are deeply involved with the Jewish-Israeli society and, in some cases, live like Jews, but who are not recognized halachically as Jews. Their main concern is about interfaith marriage within Israel. Therefore, the goal of the reform is to increase the demand for Orthodox conversion in Israel. The

---

198 For the full document see Nissim (Ibid., 62, note 160).

199 See Yoni Rothenberg, "Resistance in All Directions," *Arutz-Sheva*, June 7, 2018.

200 HCJ 11013/05, Dahan v. the Interior Minister.

201 Rodriguez-Toshbeim v. Minister of the Interior. Ibid.

core of the reform (lead by the former Minister of Religious Affairs Kahana) is to give municipal rabbis the authority to establish local conversion tribunals. The assumption is that decentralizing conversion will effect greater halachic pluralism and different standards of Orthodox conversion, and will therefore be more attractive to those non-Jews who live in Israel and are considering converting. It is worth mentioning that although the reform is minor and aims to increase the willingness of Israelis to halachically convert, it has met with immense criticism from ultraorthodox rabbis and politicians.

Summary

The Status Quo on conversion emerged as a matter of customary practice in the late 1950s, whereby only individuals who are Jewish according to Orthodox halakhah are recognized as Jews for various legal purposes; but the situation has changed significantly since then. In a long process spanning four decades, the legislature and, more importantly, the court, gave new content to the concepts of "who is a Jew" and "who is a convert." In practice, the court created a situation in which the State of Israel recognizes all types of conversion carried out by Jewish communities anywhere in the world, as well as Orthodox conversions conducted in Israel outside the chief rabbinate. However, the Status Quo survives with regard to the eligibility under the Law of Return of a Jew who belongs to another religion and has even been reiterated by an amendment to that law.[202] The recent establishment by Religious Zionist rabbis of private conversion courts demonstrates that all sectors of the Jews in Israel lack confidence that the state and its religious service agencies can provide these services properly. Here, too, the Status Quo has eroded—trimmed from the top by the High Court of Justice (forced to decide because the political system could not arrive at a consensus) and pruned from below by challenges to the state authorities.

2.4 Kashrut: The Rabbinate's Monopoly and its Disintegration

Most Jews in Israel observe kashrut (Jewish dietary laws) to some extent. Polls show that 76% of them maintain a kosher kitchen, and 70% eat only kosher

---

202 This issue was raised in the Rufeisen case (*supra* note 171).

food outside the home.[203] Accordingly, the vast majority of packaged food products sold in Israeli supermarkets are kosher. Of the ten largest chains, only one chain stocks nonkosher food.[204] Most food factories in the country produce only kosher products, and most hotels comply with the laws of kashrut.[205] In the restaurant sector, the rate is lower; estimates from recent years are that only 22% to 35% of the restaurants in Israel are kosher.[206] The Ministry of Religious Services estimates that about fifteen thousand businesses around the country, or about 80% of the food sector, have a kashrut certificate.[207]

Arrangements to supervise kashrut predate the state. The Status Quo Letter refers to the matter, but only with regard to the guarantee of kosher food supply in public kitchens. In reality, and from the 1980s on by law, the chief rabbinate monopolized kashrut certification. This situation is problematic in two respects: first, it infringes on the freedom of occupation of wish to represent their establishments as kosher but do not want to deal with the chief rabbinate; and second, it violates the religious freedom of those who adhere to halakhic standards of kashrut that vary from those promulgated by the chief rabbinate.

Here too, a process of the creation of a Status Quo, although at a relatively late date, can be identified, followed, quite recently, by its erosion.

The Early Days

As early as 1927, Knesset Yisrael—the quasi-governmental body of the Jewish community under the British Mandate—determined that local councils would be established to oversee the kashrut of the meat supply.[208] About a decade later, their jurisdiction was expanded and they began to serve as religious councils. The Status Quo Letter declares that "all the necessary means must be taken to

---

203 Asher Arian and Ayala Keissar-Sugarmen, *A Portrait of Israeli Jews: Beliefs, Observance, and Values of Jews in Israel, 2009* (Jerusalem: The Israel Democracy Institute and the AVI CHAI Foundation, 2012), 36.

204 Yoram Abramson & Co., Accountants, "Examining Kashrut Costs in Israel and the Rabbinate's Monopoly on Kosher: An Initial Draft," submitted to the Budget Division of the Ministry of Finance, June 2015, 7 [Heb.].

205 Ibid., 25.

206 For different assessments, see Eliezer Levin, "Record: 1,828 Kosher Restaurants in Israel," news1, November 25, 2010.

207 Neta Moshe, "The Kosher Food and Beverage System in Israel and an Estimation of Its Cost," Knesset Research and Information Center, January 15, 2017, 3 [Heb.].

208 This chapter is based in part on a previous study of mine: Ariel Finkelstein and Shuki Friedman, *Is This Place Kosher? Deficiencies and Proposal for Reform in the Kosher Market in Israel*, Policy Study 117 (Jerusalem: The Israel Democracy Institute, 2017), 15 [Heb.]).

ensure that every state kitchen serving Jews will be kosher."[209] Independence was followed by the Kosher Food Order for Soldiers 5708-1948, which states that "all Jewish soldiers in the Israel Defense Forces must be guaranteed kosher food." Although the letter and this law do not require that public institutions and the IDF provide kosher food exclusively, but only that kosher food be available for those who want it, in practice the kitchens of all government offices and state institutions prepare kosher food only.

In the early decades of statehood, the pre-1948 arrangement persisted and local religious councils issued kashrut certificates without formal statutory authority to do so. The prevention of fraud in the kosher sector was part of the general anti-fraud enforcement in commerce and did not constitute a separate offense.[210] It was common to see it as a section of the Criminal Law Ordinance. Starting in 1954, religious Knesset members pushed for legislation to regulate the kashrut market. The first bill, the Public Fraud Prevention (Kosher) Bill, 1959, and many that followed, did not pass the Knesset, and the kashrut sector remained unregulated for many years.[211] In other words, the Status Quo regarding kashrut was that the local rabbinate, local rabbis, and kashrut supervisors operating under the direction of local religious councils granted kashrut certificates.

The situation changed in the early 1980s with the enactment of the Israel Chief Rabbinate Law, 5740-1980, and the Prohibition of Fraud in Kashrut Law, 5743-1983.[212] These statutes granted the rabbinate a monopoly over the kosher sector in Israel. They stipulate that the Chief Rabbinate Council of Israel, rabbis approved by the chief rabbinate, and local rabbis are authorized to issue a kosher certificates to establishments that sell, prepare, or serve food, including factories, hotels, and restaurants.[213] In practice, however, it is local rabbis who grant kashrut certification. A local rabbi may do so only in the locality he serves, in concert with the local religious council (there are 131 in the country). Where there is no religious council, kashrut is overseen by the religious services

209 For the Status Quo Letter, see "The Status Quo Letter," accessed July 1, 20222, https://he.wikisource.org/wiki/%D7%9E%D7%9B%D7%AA%D7%91_%D7%94%D7%A1%D7%98%D7%98%D7%95%D7%A1_%D7%A7%D7%95%D7%95.

210 Moti Talias, "Private Kashrut in Israel: Voluntary Regulation as an Integrated Product of Supply and Demand," *Heqer ha-Hevra ha-Haredi* 2 (1990): 117, 118 [Heb.].

211 Warhaftig, *Constitution*, 289.

212 For the background of this legislation, see HCJ 6494/14, Gini v. the Chief Rabbinate (published in *Nevo*, June 6, 2016), 14.

213 Except for the IDF, where the military rabbinate has jurisdiction over kashrut.

department of the local municipality.[214] This is one of the religious councils' main, and perhaps most important, roles.

The Prohibition of Fraud in Kashrut Law authorizes the chief rabbinate to work through a dedicated enforcement unit, but does not subordinate local rabbis to the chief rabbinate.[215] Nevertheless, many circulars issued by the directors general of the Ministry of Religious Services (or its predecessors), and to some extent High Court rulings,[216] represent the chief rabbinate as the halakhic overseer of the local rabbis, though the legal authority for this determination is unclear. The chief rabbinate has been running a national kashrut department for some years and publishes halakhic procedures on kashrut.[217] In practice, however, in view of the foggy legal situation, the aspiration to turn these procedures into a national standard for granting kashrut certification has been fulfilled only in part and the degree of adherence to the rabbinate's guidelines is subject to the whims of local rabbis.[218]

Private Kashrut Bodies

Alongside the state kashrut system, there are a number of private kashrut agencies (which go under the generic name "Badatz") that provide certification to a more stringent standard (known as "mehadrin"). The agencies charge business owners a fee for providing them with kashrut inspectors. For the most part, their supervision is characterized by a greater presence of the inspectors on the premises, the use of manufactured raw materials that themselves are recognized

---

214 The issue is regulated by the Jewish Religious Services Regulations (Elections of City Rabbis), 2007. In practice, the choice of the rabbis is strongly influenced by the preference of the minister of religious services. In addition to the representatives he appoints to the electoral college, the minister indirectly controls the synagogues' representatives and in general has administrative authority that allows him to influence the outcome. See Eitan Jordan and Ariel Finkelstein, *Appointment of City Rabbis in Israel* (Jerusalem: Institute for Zionist Strategy, 2004), 26–39 [Heb.].

215 State Comptroller, *Annual Report 59 for 2008 and for Fiscal Year 2007 Accounts*, May 2009, 962.

216 HCJ 11157/03, Hospitality Golan Ltd. v. Chief Rabbinate of Israel (published in *Nevo*, Sept. 5, 2007).

217 For the history of this department, see Rabbi Isser Klonsky, "The National Kashrut Department of the Chief Rabbinate," in *The Chief Rabbinate of Israel: Seventy Years, 1921–1991: Its Powers, Activities, and History*, vol. 2, ed. Itamar Warhaftig and Rabbi Shmuel Katz (Jerusalem: Heikhal Shlomo, 5768), 687 [Heb.].

218 Aviad Bakshi and Neta Shapira, *The Kashrut System in Israel: Analysis and Proposal for Restructuring* (Jerusalem: Ecclesiastical Forum, 5776), 6–7.

as "mehadrin," and stricter requirements of various sorts.[219] In the country's first few decades, only a few Badatz agencies active. Since the 1980s, however, the field burgeoned, until there are twenty-six active Badatz organizations today,[220] most of them affiliated with ultraorthodox groups or institutions.[221]

Supreme Court Rulings and the Erosion of the Rabbinate's Monopoly

The chief rabbinate acquired a monopoly on kashrut in Israel because, according to the law, a business that represents itself as kosher but possesses kosher certification only from a private kashrut organization violates the Kashrut Fraud Prohibition Law. The law makes the chief rabbinate a monopoly, due to the legal exclusivity it gives it to oversee kashrut and the authority to enforce it and due to the fact that a business owner cannot contact another local authority in the area where he operates. But this monopoly has recently been weakened and may have even broken, again by a bottom-up insurgency and rulings by the High Court of Justice.

The combination of deficiencies in the kashrut system,[222] rabbinical misconduct, and business owners' unwillingness to pay for kashrut supervision without justification led many to advertise their establishments as kosher even in the absence of an official kashrut certificate. In 2016, a new organization, Hashgacha Pratit ("private supervision") decided to fight for the right to grant kashrut certification without the need for another certificate from the chief rabbinate. Administrative fines issued the chief rabbinate against a business that used this service led to the Gini case, which seems to be curtailing the chief rabbinate's monopoly.

Gini, a Jerusalem restaurateur, complied with the laws of kashrut and presented his establishment as kosher, but did not have a certificate from the rabbinate. After he was fined by the rabbinate's enforcement unit for kashrut fraud, he petitioned for cancellation of the fine, on the grounds that he was in fact operating a kosher business, even without the rabbinate's confirmation,

219 State Comptroller (*supra* note 215), 990.

220 See the remarks by Ron Chacham of the Tax Authority at a hearing of the Knesset State Control Committee, minutes of session eighty-six of the State Control Committee, twentieth Knesset (February 16, 2016), 46.

221 For a comprehensive study of the activities of the Badatz kashrut agencies in Israel, see Talias (*supra* note 210), 117–146.

222 See Finkelstein and Friedman (*supra* note 208), 38, 60.

and was entitled to represent his restaurant as kosher. After two years, the High Court of Justice issued a majority opinion that the Kashrut Fraud Act does indeed grant the rabbinate a monopoly on the kosher market; hence the owner must obtain a certificate from the rabbinate in order to advertise a business as kosher.[223] The petitioners sought an additional hearing by the court.

After the additional hearing, and as part of the decision to reject the appeal, Chief Justice Miriam Naor ruled that the correct interpretation of the Prohibition of Kashrut Fraud Law was not that of the original panel. The new decision agreed that the rabbinate does have a monopoly on the word "kosher" and a business must not represent itself as kosher without a certificate from the rabbinate. It may, however, offer a truthful representation of the steps it takes to ensure that the food it serves is kosher.[224]

This ruling is vague and subject to interpretation. According to the chief rabbinate's interpretation, any action that constitutes a "kosher representation" that is not merely a business owner's statement of his kosher policy, but that of an organization that issues a kashrut certificate displayed by the business, even via this loophole, is kashrut fraud. In light of this interpretation, the rabbinate has fined a business that displayed a kashrut certificate from Hashgacha Pratit.[225] On the other hand, the petitioners and organizations that wish to issue kashrut certificates without the rabbinate's approval believe that the ruling permit them to do so, thus breaking the chief rabbinate's monopoly. The petitioners' interpretation, which seems to me more correct, in tandem with the dynamics of the kashrut market, create a new reality that erodes the rabbinate's monopoly.

Relying on the High Court's ruling, in early 2018 Tzohar set up a private kashrut supervision system to compete with the chief rabbinate.[226] The organization said that it hoped to gain a 10% market share within three years.[227] As far as is known, the chief rabbinate has yet to fine businesses with a Zohar kashrut certificate, thus effectively acquiescing in the situation for now.

---

223 See the Gini case (*supra* note 212). The ruling was preceded by a dispute among government officials. Then-Attorney General Yehuda Weinstein held that, under the constitutional right freedom of occupation and the principles of legal interpretation, the Kashrut Fraud Prohibition Act does not require an owner to obtain a rabbinate kashrut certificate to present the business as kosher. The chief rabbinate's position was that the law gives it a monopoly on kashrut market and that representation of a business as kosher without its certificate is illegal. Both positions were brought before the court.

224 HCJ 5026/16, Gini v. Chief Rabbinate of Israel (published in *Nevo*, September 12, 2017).

225 Ora Koren, "The Rabbinate Answers the High Court: We Fined a Business that Displayed an Alternative Kosher Certificate," *TheMarker*, September 26, 2017.

226 Hanan Greenwood, "'Revolution': Tzohar Launches a Kashrut System," *Israel Today*, February 26, 2018.

227 See the Tzohar website: https://www.tzohar.org.il/?page_id=16250.

The kashrut reform of 2021: as a result of the inefficiency and growing criticism of the chief rabbinate kashrut system, the Bennet government promoted a reform within the kashrut market in Israel. The reform was motivated by the bottom-up pressure and the High Court of Justice's decisions. In practice, it adopted the idea that kashrut can be given by private organizations and, therefore, breach the chief rabbinate kashrut monopoly. According to the reform, the chief rabbinate will remain only a regulator of the kashrut market. It will set the kashrut standards and will give license to private kashrut organizations that will replace the chief rabbinate's supplying of kashrut services.

Summary

In the field of kashrut, too, a combination of court rulings and bottom-up activities by organizations has produced a significant erosion of the chief rabbinate's monopoly over the kosher food market in Israel. In this case, the pressure applied by these two players led the government to implement reform in the kashrut market that in many ways adopts the de facto situation into a kashrut amended law.

4

Religion and State: The Failed Attempts to Enact Arrangements

In the seventy-four years since the establishment of the state, major energy has been invested in attempts to reach religious-secular consensus on issues of religion and state. But they have not produced any tangible result, and the battle over the Jewish character of the state continues.

The attempts at compromise arrangements have two main axes: legislation, especially at the national level, and proposals for "soft" regulation under the auspices of a social compact or covenant.

The Failure to Resolve Religion and State Issues through Legislation

As we saw in the last chapter, ever since 1948, and even more so in recent decades, with the increased clout of the ultraorthodox parties the ability to achieve a political consensus on issues of religion and state has been very limited. By way of illustration, 471 bills dealing with aspects of these issues (Shabbat, marriage and divorce, kashrut, conversion) were submitted to the Knesset between 2000 and 2016,[1] but almost no important bill became law.

1 According to the Knesset website, there were 80 bills dealing with Shabbat, 133 with kashrut, 36 with conversion, 172 with marriage, and 50 with divorce.

The only significant changes during those years regarded conversion, with a government decision to allow local rabbis to set up conversion courts;[2] but the decision was reversed by the next government, which did not include the ultraorthodox parties.[3] Another change was the opening of the marriage registration districts and the authorization of the Tzohar rabbinical organization to register marriage applications, which put it into competition with the registration offices run by local religious councils and made the service more efficient.[4] Finally, as mentioned above,[5] due to pressure by the ultraorthodox parties, in early 2018 the Hours of Work and Rest Law and the Municipalities Ordinance were amended, but in a way that does not resolve or regulate the Shabbat issue.

There are several reasons for the continuing failure to reach an agreement on any religion and state issue by means of legislation or regulation. A major factor, even when the proposed rules were close to the positions of the religious and ultraorthodox parties, is the rabbis' stubborn resistance. They have rejected even the slightest compromise and made it impossible to come to any agreement about core issues of religion and state relations.

To illustrate the rabbis' rigid attitudes, I will analyze two significant attempts that ultimately failed. From a historical perspective, had the attempts succeed they could have prevented the erosion of the Status Quo on the religious side, thereby preserving the Jewish image of the state, as the Orthodox demand: (1) the attempt to enact the Shabbat Law between 1957 and 1965; and (2) then-MK Nahum Langenthal's initiative for comprehensive regulation of religion and state issues in 1999.

---

2 See Jonathan Less, "Netanyahu's U-turn: The Government Approves the Softer Version of the Conversion Reform," *Ha'aretz*, Nov. 2, 2014. The passage of the reform by means of a government decision rather than legislation was also the result of political compromise, due to fear of the ultraorthodox. The decision is based on a proposal by the Israel Democracy Institute and Itim, formulated in the bill sponsored by MK Elazar Stern. See Yedidia Z. Stern, Shaul Farber, and Elad Kaplan, *Proposal for a State Conversion Law* (Jerusalem: The Israel Democracy Institute and Itim Association, 2014).

3 See Yair Ettinger, "Government Approves: Conversion Reform Will Be Revoked and the Rabbinical Courts Will Be Transferred to the Ministry of Religion," *Ha'aretz*, July 5, 2015.

4 The Law to Amend the Marriage and Divorce Ordinance (Registration) (Registration Areas), 2009, passed its third reading on October 29, 2013. See also Omri Nachmias and Yaki Adamker "Tzohar Law Is Approved: Couples Can Choose Where to Marry," *Walla!* Oct. 29, 2013, https://news.walla.co.il/item/2689844.

5 *Supra*, 70.

Warhaftig's Shabbat Bills

As mentioned, the issue of Shabbat rest and the public sphere was already controversial when the state was born. The issue was debated even before the first government was formed; it was agreed in its basic rules that legislation would be enacted to stipulate that the Shabbat and Jewish holidays would be the official days of rest.[6] Justice Minister Pinchas Rosen stated that this principle would be enshrined in the details of the Shabbat rest legislation.[7] The first step towards regulating Shabbat rest was the Hours of Work and Rest Law, 5701-1951,[8] but this law did not satisfy the religious parties. Seeing it as a social law, they sought legislation with a declarative character of the religious character of Shabbat.

The negotiations about such a Shabbat law were renewed before the establishment of the seventh government in 1944;[9] Ben-Gurion promised the Hapoel Hamizrachi party that "a Shabbat rest law would be enacted." When this did not happen and a private member's bill sponsored by Warhaftig did not pass,[10] the coalition agreement for the establishment of the tenth government (1961) incorporated the demand by the National Religious Party (the successor of Hapoel Hamizrachi) for enactment of a Shabbat law.[11]

Its text was by nature a compromise between the religious party's desire to enshrine the religious character of the Shabbat in the State of Israel and the secular parties' desire to curtail the law's religious dimension as much as possible and permit a reasonable level of activity on the Shabbat. The proposed law was not passed, and the Hours of Work and Rest Law was amended instead.[12] The government, led by Ben-Gurion, was in no hurry to honor its commitment to the NRP; but in addition, the chief rabbinate and many rabbis who opposed the proposed law were a major factor in its demise. Warhaftig described the situation as follows:

> Quite a factor in pausing, hesitating, and the tedious negotiations was the Chief Rabbinate's negative position on the "Fragmented

---

6 See Shabbat Rest Law (Ibid., 32, note 29), 6.
7 Warhaftig, *Constitution*, 266, according to *Knesset Record* (Ibid., 28, note 26), 1753.
8 *Supra*, 26.
9 Nov. 3, 1955.
10 The Shabbat and Holidays of Israel Bill (Prohibition of Business Activity), 1959. See Shabbat Rest Law (Ibid., 32, note 29), 17.
11 Warhaftig, *Constitution*, 268.
12 See above on page 30.

> Shabbat" law. I did a lot to explain the situation to the Chief Rabbinate and to the Israeli rabbis in general.... We did not ask the Chief Rabbinate for consent... All we wanted was a lack of resistance, retroactive approval, and we didn't get it.[13]

The bill envisioned by the coalition agreement and that Warhaftig, when he served as minister of religious affairs, submitted on his own as a proposed Basic Law, was based on the Status Quo as it existed then. But it would also have expanded the restrictions on economic activity on Shabbat, with a countrywide ban on commercial operations, including cinemas and theaters, and limits on restaurants and cafes (reduced opening hours and no music). But it would not have imposed a total ban and would have allowed, by implication, cultural and sports activity on Shabbat, and public transportation in Haifa.[14] The explanatory notes noted that the underlying Jewish religious basis of the proposed law rests and announced that its purpose "was to prevent the undermining of the days of rest in the State of Israel."[15]

Although the law was drafted by someone who could be called the legislator of religious laws in the State of Israel, it received a cold shoulder from the chief rabbinate and many other rabbis. Although it was clear that passage of the law, with its broad scope and normative status, would strengthen public observance of the Shabbat beyond symbolic recognition, the rabbis saw only the negative aspects. They saw no religious legitimacy for even the slightest compromise about Shabbat's rest. Not willing to grant even tacit consent, they embarked on a fight against the legislation.[16]

The rabbis' bitter resistance to any compromise on the Shabbat (and on other issues) derived from their inability to deviate from halakhah, even when the purpose and political outcome would be positive from their perspective. They held that they represented the word of God and eternal law of the Torah, which cannot change and become flexible in response to national politics. Hence even rabbis who considered supporting the Shabbat bill or who did not express strong opposition to it initially came to oppose it, due to pressure by more extreme rabbis, leaving only a few of their number still in favor of a compromise.

---

13 In this context, Warhaftig cites a letter by Rabbi Yehezkel Abramsky, one of the leading halakhic decisors at the time, in which the rabbi make it clear that he opposes the law "because it includes concessions that cannot be made" (Warhaftig, *Constitution*, 271).

14 The Shabbat Rest Law (Ibid., note 29), 33, explanatory notes.

15 The proposed Basic Law: Shabbat and Jewish Festivals (Prohibition of Business Activity), 1964 (see Shabbat Rest Law [*supra* note 68, 28]).

16 Warhaftig, *Constitution*, 271.

Because the relevant halakhic rulings[17] and political dynamics about this matter are typical of broader issue, I will discuss them briefly here.

The core of the halakhic debate focused on two lacunae in the bill that the rabbis could not countenance: the lack of any reference to Shabbat observance in agriculture and the tacit consent to continuing the operation of public transportation on Shabbat in Haifa. The latter is why Yehoshua Kaniel, the chief rabbi of Haifa, was one of the most prominent opponents. The campaign against the bill and the compromises it entailed was led by Ashkenazi Chief Rabbi Yitzchak Isaac Halevi.

His general opposition to the bill as a matter of principle was highlighted in a letter he sent to Warhaftig, which began as follows: "I have looked into the matter with due care and I am quick to say that no such or similar law can satisfy even the minimum requirements of the rabbinate. The fact that agriculture in parks and fields is not mentioned is enough to condemn it." Rabbi Herzog went on to note that the only halakhically acceptable excuse for Sabbath desecration was a threat to human life. Because the proposed law would permit Sabbath desecration in other situations, he must oppose it.[18]

The opposition to the bill was formulated in detail in a pamphlet by Rabbi Yaakov Aryeh Plavnik of Haifa.[19] The arguments advanced in it were adopted as the official position of the Haifa City and District Rabbinical Committee and endorsed by other leading rabbis. The halakhic debate about continuation of the Status Quo (allowing public transportation in Haifa) revolved around the question of "sacrificing one person for another"; that is, is it permitted to "sacrifice" one person—in the sense of life and death or in other respects—in order to save many others?

The issue of "one person for another" appears in several contexts in the halakhic sources. In one of them, the debate is about whether the women of a city are permitted to hand over one of their number to hostile gentiles, knowing that she will be raped, so as to save the other women from that fate. The Mishnah rules that they must all submit to the gentiles and be raped and

---

17 Rabbi Avraham Wasserman, too, suggested seeing this issue as an interesting case study of how rabbis rule on political issues related to questions of religious and state ("Status-Quo Halakhah," *Pri Etz Hagan* 3 [2003], 147).

18 Rabbi Yitzchak Isaac Halevi Herzog, *Legislation for Israel according to the Torah*, vol. 2 (Jerusalem: Mosad Hav Kook and Yad Harav Herzog, 5765), 101. However, Rabbi Herzog leaves Warhaftig and his fellow politicians some room to maneuver.

19 Rabbi Ya'akov Aryeh Plavnik, *A Truncated Shabbat Law According to Halakhah*, parts 1–2 (Haifa: The Rabbinical Committee of the Chief Rabbinate of Haifa and the District, 5723–5724). The opinion of the chief rabbi of Haifa, as well as the approbations of major rabbis for the positions expressed by Plavnik, also appeared in this publication.

cannot save themselves by handing over one individual.[20] Similarly, the Tosefta states that if the inhabitants of a city are ordered to deliver one of themselves, otherwise all of them will be killed, it is better for all of them to die and not save themselves in this way.[21] It is forbidden to sacrifice one individual, even if this results in wholesale slaughter or rape. Accordingly, the opponents of the bill argued, giving up the Sabbath in Haifa to strengthen it in other places would be tantamount to saving the lives of many at the cost of sacrificing the life of one individual or the innocence (and in fact dignity and life) of one woman—and thus forbidden.[22]

The very choice of this analogy between the Shabbat desecration of a few "in exchange for" preventing the desecration of many, and issues pertaining to an individual life as opposed to many, illustrates that the rabbis chose to regard the issue as a matter of life and death and treat it with the greatest possible stringency. Furthermore, in their rulings, the rabbis ignored many nuances found in the halakhic discourse about such difficult cases and painted the result in stark black-and-white terms. Ignoring this complexity allowed them to cite these sources to strengthen their position about the severity of the halakhic concession embodied in the Shabbat bill.[23]

Several rabbis, mainly from religious Zionist circles, did come out in support of the bill. Prominent among them was Rabbi Shaul Israeli,[24] who argued, in an incisive halakhic discussion, that the halakhic analogy employed by the bill's opponents was fundamentally flawed, both halakhically and logically. From a

---

20 M *Terumot* 8:12: "So too women who were told by gentiles: Give us one of you to be defiled, and if not, we will defile all of you, they should all be defiled and not hand over even one soul from Israel."

21 T *Terumot* 7:13: "A group of people who have been told by foreigners: Give us one of you to be killed; and if not, we will kill all of you; they should allow themselves to be killed and not hand over even one soul from Israel."

22 Rabbi Kaniel compares Shabbat desecration "only" to the rape of a woman by Gentiles. See Plavnik (*supra* note 19), part 1, 4. Plavnik inflates the halakhic ban and cites other cases that balance one life against many (for example, part 1, 12–13, et passim), which, as stated, was backed by the Haifa rabbis.

23 Rabbi Wasserman shows that even if you accept this analogy fundamentally, the halakhic result can be different. See Wasserman (*supra* note 17), 149.

24 Rabbi of Kfar Haroeh and later the dean of the Merkaz Harav Yeshiva, a judge of the Supreme Rabbinical Court and member of the Chief Rabbinate Council, who dealt extensively with halakhah and policy issues. It is interesting to note that Rabbi Yisraeli entitled one article "Laws of Coalition," in which he demonstrates his understanding of the political need to be flexible and compromise. See the article in: Yehuda Shaviv, ed., *At the Junction of Torah and State: Selected Articles from the Torah and State Files, Re-edited*, vol. 2 (Alon Shvut: Zomet Institute, 5751), 116; Rabbi Shaul Israeli, *Amud Hayemini* (Jerusalem: The Torah and the State Institute, 5760), chapter 11.

halakhic point of view, the cases were not at all similar; and logically, whereas the cases cited banned hands-on action—delivering an individual to hostile gentiles—the case of Haifa's buses involved only the maintenance of the current situation and was ultimately a sacrifice of lesser severity.

The rabbinical politics that affect rulings about issues of religion and state are also interesting. The Shabbat question was addressed by every rabbi who dealt with and ruled with them. The Warhaftig bills of the late 1950s and the later effort to enact a Shabbat law in the early 1960s provoked great controversy among rabbis. Some strongly opposed them, while others offered tacit or active support. However, as the debate grew more impassioned and it became more likely that the bill would pass, the supporters' voices faded and it was the opponents who set the tone.

An illustration of this dynamic can be found in the deliberations of the Chief Rabbinate Council[25] about Warhaftig's later proposal. The public debate can be tracked in the columns of *Hatzofeh,* the daily affiliated with Warhaftig's National Religious Party. According to these reports, although some members of the council did not oppose the compromise,[26] the chief rabbi of Haifa and other opponents eventually triumphed and the rabbis' public voice denounced the bill.[27]

From a historical perspective, and as can be seen above in the section on the Shabbat, for those interested in a more religious character for the Shabbat in Israel this was a missed opportunity to pass a law that might have prevented some of the later developments on this front.

---

25 At the time, this body had a greater halakhic weight than it has today and was more widely accepted as a decisive actor in public religious controversies. See, for example, Y. N. Hakohen, "The Shabbat Law," *Hatzofeh,* April 26, 1962. He wrote that due to the dispute between the rabbis, which is at its core a halakhic dispute, adoption of a Shabbat law must be conditional on a decision by the Chief Rabbinate Council.

26 See, for example, M. Ben Shlomo, "Today the Chief Rabbinate Council Will Discuss the Shabbat Bill Agreed to in the Coalition Negotiations," *Hatzofeh,* Aug. 1, 1962.

27 In 1964, D. Zeira summarized the Shabbat Law affair on the pages of *Hatzofeh:* "The Shabbat law, whose passage by Fifth Knesset was agreed to when the Government was established more than three years ago, is a 'bill' that still has been presented for payment because of the partial opposition within the religious camp. is clear that on such a controversial principle—which requires a halakhic and public decision—we do not follow the majority and one does not ignore a minority opinion. It is not the number of those who argue for or against the law that counts, but the number of arguments and counter-arguments" ("The Shabbat Limit," *Hatzofeh,* November 20, 1964).

The Attempt to Regulate Religion and State Relations in the Early 2000s—and Its Failure

In 1999, when Nahum Langenthal of the National Religious Party (NRP) was elected to the Knesset, he decided to focus on producing a comprehensive agreement on religion and state relations in Israel.[28] Langenthal formulated a proposal that expressed components of the Status Quo in religion and state relations and to which the ultraorthodox and Orthodox rabbis, as well as leaders of the secular camp, could accept. The innovation was that the proposal sought to encompass all the major issues of religion and state relations in Israel, producing a series of internal balances on the issues[29] and compromises that both rabbis and secular leaders could agree to.[30] On some issues, the proposal included new legislation[31] that later served as the basis for the Gavison-Medan Covenant and other documents.

Understanding the issue's extreme sensitivity for the rabbis and secular Knesset members on both the right and left, Langenthal worked in close coordination with leading religious Zionist rabbis in search of a consensus. As part of the process, he shared the proposal with rabbis of the ultraorthodox United Torah Judaism party. After several months of work he achieved a broad consensus on almost all issues of religion and state relations.

But this historic opportunity to set religion and state relations in order was also missed. After Langenthal published the text of his bill, cosponsored by eighteen Knesset members from most factions, internal opposition surfaced motion within the NRP itself. Knesset members who opposed the proposal presented it in a negative light to former chief rabbis Avraham Shapira and

---

28 Due Disclosure: I served as MK Langenthal's advisor in those days and took part in forging the agreements and writing the bill.

29 See Gideon Alon, "The NRP Legislative Initiative: Public Transportation on Shabbat," *Ha'aretz*, Feb. 16, 2000.

30 The proposal's sections deal with the following topics: Shabbat and Jewish holidays; marriage and divorce; conversion; religious services in Israel; kashrut; the rabbinical courts; Jewish heritage and culture; *mishpat ivri*. It also calls for the establishment of "The 'Together' Council" to serve as the framework for dialogue among the various sectors of Israeli society and as an advisory body to the government and the Knesset on religious and state issues. See Nachum Langenthal, "Religion and State Bill, 2000," in *Shevet Achim: Religious-Secular Relations, Attitudes, Proposals, Beliefs*, ed. Uri Dromi (Jerusalem: The Israel Democracy Institute, 2005), 317.

31 Social compacts that preceded the proposal dealt with issues of religion and state, but not at the same scope and level of detail.

Mordechai Eliyahu. Their rejection of the bill caused other rabbis, including Rabbi Yaakov Ariel to renege on their promised support. The bill was shelved.[32]

Later, Langenthal and other MKs submitted a bill that dealt only with the Shabbat, which would prohibit commercial activity but permit limited leisure activity and public transportation. This bill, too, had the tacit or active consent of rabbis, as well as a Knesset member of the Shas faction, who relied on the opinion of Rabbi Ovadia Yosef.[33] Once again, the opponents raised an outcry and the supporters eventually pulled back out of fear of them.[34]

Proposals for Informal Regulation of Religion and State Relations

Beginning in the late 1980s, due to the continuing sense of crisis in religious-secular relations in Israel, various public groups initiated discussions about the growing rift in society, including religion and state issues. The first document produced by these groups was the Jewish-Social Convention of the Religious Kibbutz (1987), which dealt mainly with Shabbat issues, marriage and divorce, and the attitude towards the non-Orthodox Jewish movements. A few years later, Prof. Ruth Gavison and Rabbi Yoel Bin-Nun hosted a conference on the Shabbat (1996). In the late 1990s, the moderate religious Meimad party and Knesset members Alex Lubotzky and Yossi Beilin cooperated on a comprehensive document that dealt with most religion and state issues and had some public resonance (1998). In the late 1990s and early 2000s, the Israel Democracy Institute sponsored a Constitution by Consensus project, which involved participants from all sectors of Israeli society (2003).[35] Other documents that have enjoyed some public attention and that dealt with religion and state relations include the Kinneret Covenant (2001), the result of the

---

32 Interview with Nachum Langenthal, Aug. 27, 2017.

33 See Dalia Shechori, "Proposal for a 'Shabbat Law' to Prohibit Trade and Allow Entertainment," *Ha'aretz*, December 31, 2001.

34 Rabbi Mordechai Eliyahu stated that "Pharaoh himself would reject a deal or compromise on the Shabbat law." Rabbi Avraham Shapira opposed the law, because "no deals are made about the Shabbat." See Anshel Pfeiffer, "The NRP Rabbis Also Oppose Langenthal's Shabbat Law," *Ha'aretz*, Jan. 2,.2002. See also the op-ed by Yair Sheleg, which focuses on the opportunity missed by the refusal to compromise about the Shabbat, "The Fight for Nuance" *Ha'aretz*, January 22, 2002.

35 The results of these discussions were published. See Meir Shamgar et al., *Constitution by Consent: A Proposal by the Israeli Democracy Institute* (Jerusalem: The Israel Democracy Institute, 2005), 92.

discussions of the National Responsibility Forum, and the Israel Internal Peace Convention whose founders included several senior politicians.[36]

In the mid-1990s, after the assassination of Yitzhak Rabin, Prof. Ruth Gavison and Rabbi Yaakov Medan launched a lengthy dialogue that eventually led to the Gavison-Medan Covenant (2003).[37] This document seems to have been the most prominent of all these attempts; in the years since its publication it has continued to serve as an inspiration or even the basis for concrete arrangement to regulate religion and state relations. This was reflected in attempts by Knesset members to enact the entire covenant or some of its clauses, given that the general public can identify with its principles and seems willing to accept it as a compromise solution.[38]

Why did such documents emerge as a major tool for regulating religion and state relations? Could they be effective?

Asher Cohen offers an explanation for the proliferation of such covenants.[39] According to him, after three decades when Israeli politics followed the model of consensual democracy, in the 1980s it was replaced by the model of crisis democracy, due to the consolidation of two opposing political blocs. With regard to religion and state, the consensual model was characterized by an attempt to tolerate pluralism and to avoid decisions that would force the minority to act counter to its values. On the other hand, in a politics of crisis, marked by partisan rivalry and a tense balance of power, extremists have greater weight and can try to impose decisions related to values. So after religion and state relations were governed through the political system in the first decades of the state, starting in the 1980s, when the ability to reach a compromise diminished, the public felt a need to draft covenants in order to regulate the matter through compromise.

Another possible explanation for the inability to reach a decision on religion and state issues through the political system is the rise of the ultraorthodox and more extreme religious parties. As a result of the advent of Shas in the 1980s, ultraorthodox representation in the Knesset increased. In addition,

---

36 For a review of the various religion and state compacts, see Tova Ilan and Batya Kahana-Dror, eds., *Compacts in Israel: Attempts to Arrange Secular and Religious Relations* (Jerusalem: The Yachad Council affiliated with the President's Residence, Jerusalem, 5765).

37 Ruth Gavison and Ya'acov Medan, *Basis for a New Social Covenant between the Observant and the Secular in Israel* (Jerusalem: The Israel Democracy Institute and AVI CHAI, 2003).

38 For example, according to a survey by the Coalition for an Israeli Shabbat, 63% of the nonreligious in Israel support regulation of the Shabbat issue on the basis of the Gavison-Medan Compact. See Orly Goldkling and Gideon Dukov, "In Keeping with Religious Law," *Makor Rishon*, Oct. 6, 2016.

39 Asher Cohen, "Compacts to Regulate Secular and Religious Relations: Public Attempts in Light of the Political Failure," in Dromi (*supra* note 30), 367.

along with their growing power and involvement in the management of national affairs, the ultraorthodox see themselves as protecting not only their sectoral interests but also as protecting Israel's Jewish identity. Unlike all other actors in the political arena—secular ideologues, traditionists, and the liberal Orthodox—the ultraorthodox are willing to invest all their political resources in religion and state issues, to the point of bringing down a government and forcing new elections.[40] This explains why even the thirty-third government (March 2013 to May 2015), which did not include the ultraorthodox and could have enacted arrangements reflecting the positions of the majority of the Jews in Israel, did not do so; Prime Minister Netanyahu apparently feared that he would lose any possibility of recruiting the ultraorthodox to a future coalition and that the current government or a future government headed by him would disintegrate.[41] This situation has led individuals and civil society organizations to devise consensual solutions in informal frameworks, in the hope that they could serve as a model or inspiration for politicians.

It is hard to offer a clear answer about these documents' influence on religion and state arrangements. On the one hand, the facts speak for themselves: to date, none of their proposals (including those of the Gavison-Medan Covenant, despite its wide public support) have become law. On the other hand, given the erosion of the Status Quo and the chaotic attempts to find a solution for religion and state issues, these documents are clearly important and influential. The multitude of actors involved in the issues and the inability to regulate them give these covenants moral and social validity; they become a compass and source of inspiration for leaders pursuing a compromise on religion and state issues. To give one extraparliamentary example, Supreme Court rulings have cited the Gavison-Medan Covenant as a source of inspiration.[42] In the absence of any formal arrangement on the horizon, these documents have practical importance, so this course of action may prove to be relevant and fruitful in the future as well.

---

40 Traditionally, Hapoel Hamizrachi and then the NRP were the protectors of the state's Jewish character, to the point of bringing down the first Rabin government in 1976 over desecration of the Shabbat caused by the ceremony when the air force received its first F-15 aircraft.

41 Neri Horowitz, "The Haredim and the Supreme Court: The Conflict in Historical Perspective," *Kivunim hadashim* 5 (5762): 22, 59.

42 See, for example, para. 72 of the verdict in *Gini* case (Ibid., 76, note 224); and Justice Rubinstein's opinion in *Bremer* (Ibid., 39, note 81).

5

Factors that Erode the Status Quo

At the beginning of the study, I briefly pointed to a series of factors that led to the erosion of the Status Quo. I then showed how the Status Quo on central issues of religion and state has been eroded: the Shabbat, marriage and divorce, conversion, and kashrut. As part of the discussion of the various issues I also addressed causes of the erosion of existing legal arrangements. In this chapter I will examine this erosion through the prism of the key factors of change and characterize them from a broad perspective. I will focus on four of the factors I have listed as causing the erosion of the Status Quo: Supreme Court rulings; the transfer of religion and state arrangements to local governments; the rise of the traditionist sector of Israeli society; and the activities of civil society organizations that promote greater pluralism in religious services in Israel and express the growing desire of Jews in Israel to choose the religious services that suit their concept of Judaism.

The High Court Tries to Avoid Deciding: Judicial Rulings on Religion and State

In the chapters on the erosion of religion and state arrangements I noted the central role of the Supreme Court, sitting as the High Court of Justice, in changing and shaping the arrangements. In all the issues reviewed, the court is the dominant and often the only institution that triggers changes in the arrangements, usually the erosion of the Status Quo in the liberal direction. To judge by the broad span of judicial activism, the High Court has not refrained from issuing decisions on religion and state issues, even those that were clearly controversial. So it is not surprising that the Supreme Court has been fiercely criticized by conservative and Orthodox factions. They perceive the court as pursuing an agenda that forces liberal values onto Judaism, against the will of politicians and the Israeli public. Rabbis who see the court as an agent of secularism imposing liberal positions on the ultraorthodox sector and the Jewish state express sharp opposition. For example: "At every opportunity the High Court justices continue not only to rule justly but also to shape standards of life that are derived from their personal view. In most cases, this runs counter to the standards of life accepted by the majority of the public."[43]

Over the past three decades, we have witnessed a campaign by the ultraorthodox and religious conservatives against the High Court with regard to religion and state issues. Its peak may have been the "Demonstration by Half a Million," a protest initiated by the Gerrer rebbe and ultraorthodox politicians in 1999, in reaction to a series of Supreme Court rulings[44] that the ultraorthodox perceived as threatening their way of life and the Jewish character of the state.[45] Religious conservatives also wage war on the Supreme Court, seeing its involvement in issues of religion and state as usually favoring the secular side, trespassing on the political system, and forcing liberal secular positions on the public.[46] In 2018, the political effort to enact an "override clause" that would limit the power of the Supreme Court grew in intensity. Supporters of the proposal argue that one of its purposes is to prevent the court from destroying the Jewish character of the state.[47]

---

43 Moshe Akiva Druck, "The High Court Against the Supreme Rabbinical Court," *Hamodi'a*, December 9, 1994.

44 Rulings on the military conscription of yeshiva students, on the appointment of non-Orthodox members of religious councils, and that the rabbinical courts must divide property between a divorcing couple according to civil law and not halakhah (see Evelyn Gordon, "The Creeping Delegitimization of Freedom of Expression," *Techelet* 7 [5759]: 27).

45 Horowitz (Ibid., 88, note 41), 62–63.

46 For example, Rabbi Eliezer Melamed made frequent harsh attacks on the Supreme Court, such as: "The Damages caused by the Supreme Court. It decided that the Broadcast Authority would work on Saturday. It violated the sanctity of the family by granting status to forms of forbidden unions. . . . These are only a few examples of the court's severe infringement of the Jewish character of the state" ("Without the High Court," *Yeshiva*, 16 Kislev 5668 [Dec. 16, 2007], https://www.yeshiva.org.il/midrash/6508).

47 See Yehuda Wald, "The Override Clause: A Jewish Interest," *Arutz* 7, May 7, 2018, https://www.inn.co.il/news/523537. See also Yisrael Cohen, "The Override Clause Suits the Haredim," *Ha'aretz*, Apr. 9, 2018, https://www.haaretz.co.il/opinions/.premium-1.5980773:

Why did the Supreme Court choose the riskier activist path that threatens to erode its legitimacy for large sectors of Israeli society?[48] I suggest that the Supreme Court has been pushed into a corner and feels that, given the pervasive political paralysis on issues of religion and state, it has no alternative and must decide.[49] As I will illustrate below, even when the Supreme Court has had to issue rulings that have significant implications for religion and state relations, it has made considerable efforts to avoid them. Before ruling, the court gave the other branches of government every opportunity to make a decision themselves—and sometimes even begged them to do so. But when those efforts were stymied and it was clear that the political paralysis made it impossible for the legislature and executive to decide, the court shouldered the burden and issued its controversial decisions.

I will give examples of three of the issues I reviewed above, all of them are recent: the recognition of private Orthodox conversions, the opening of supermarkets in Tel Aviv on Shabbat,[50] and the kashrut supervisor case.[51]

Private Orthodox Conversions

One issue that the court has repeatedly tried to sidestep is conversion. Some of the High Court's rulings[52] about "who is a convert" were issued only after lengthy hearings and repeated appeals to the legislature and the government to

---

"The truth must be told: The ultra-Orthodox have no greater enemy than the rule of the High Court—precisely the Supreme Court, which was supposed to defend minorities. As those who often fight against a predatory majority, it is precisely the ultra-Orthodox who could have expected protection the judiciary to protect them against government tyranny. However, the sad reality is that every issue that is dear to halakhah and important to the ultra-Orthodox is trampled on by the justices of the Supreme Court."

48 According to the 2016 Democracy Index published by the Israel Democracy Institute, 62.5% of all Jewish Israelis have confidence in the Supreme Court, only 6% of the ultraorthodox do. See Tamar Herman, Ella Heller, Hanan Cohen, Dana Bublil, and Fadi Omar, *The Israeli Democracy Index 2016* (Jerusalem: The Israel Democracy Institute, 2016), 185.

49 "No alternative" is of course a relative matter. Critics of judicial activism argue that the court's willingness to usurp the role place of other governmental agencies in almost every area is the result of a legal policy based on a consistent worldview. This view holds that the Supreme Court is subject to almost no institutional restrictions on intervention on these issues and many others. See Shachar Lifshitz and Gideon Sapir, "Who Decides 'Who is a Jew?' On the Shalit Affair and the Proper Role of the Court in a Democratic Society," *Mehqerei Mishpat* 22, no. 2 (2004): 269, 315; Gavison (Ibid., 15, note 2), 656.

50 *General Association of Merchants and the Self-Employed* (Ibid., 39, note 82), as well as the additional hearing in the High Court (Ibid., 39, note 84).

51 HCJ 3336/04, The Movement for Governance v. the Chief Rabbinate Council (published in *Nevo*, May 9, 2017).

52 See above, 89.

decide on these issues themselves.[53] Even today, petitions on the matter remain pending for many years and the court refrains from ruling. This is evident in its dallying in the Rogachova case.[54] The petition was filed in 2006, but the ruling was not issued until March 2016. It is true that legal proceedings often last much longer than is desirable and proper, but this case seems to be truly Dickensian. Furthermore, a review of the judgment shows that the court judges made considerable efforts to avoid having to rule. The court itself admitted this in its description of the course of events: "It has been a long time since the first petition was filed in our case. The reason for the delay lies in trying to find a solution to the problem raised in the petition outside the courtroom. In this context, attempts were made to solve the individual problems raised by the petitioners."[55]

In 2011, the court wrote, in an interim decision, that "[w]e are of the opinion that the issues raised in the three petitions before us and in other petitions submitted by applicants to join (the World Association for Progressive Judaism, the Movement for Progressive Judaism, and the Masorti Movement in Israel) should be submitted to the government that will be established."[56]

The court goes on to describe the continuing saga of political negotiations, discussions within government ministries, and by the government itself, and bills submitted to the Knesset—all of these typical of religion and state issues—before concluding that "there is no escape, therefore, from a judicial decision."[57]

The Tel Aviv Municipal Bylaw on Shabbat Commerce

As stated above,[58] after the court ruled[59] that the Tel Aviv Municipality must enforce the ban on commercial activity on Saturdays, the municipality amended its bylaw and sent it for approval by the interior minister as required. The minister of the interior did not take action within the prescribed timeframe and left the matter hanging. The Tel Aviv Municipality petitioned the High Court to force him decide. As can be seen from the time that elapsed between the filing

53 The petitions by the Movement for Progressive Judaism and the Masorti Movement (HCJ 11013/05, Dahan v. the Interior Minister) calling for recognition of non-Orthodox conversions conducted in Israel were filed seventeen years ago.

54 Ibid., 69, note 196.

55 Ibid., 4.

56 Ibid.

57 Ibid., section 5 of the ruling.

58 *Supra* 50.

59 *Bremer* (*supra* note 42).

of the petition and the court's ruling, and especially from the court's attempts to get the government to state its position on the law, it is clear that the justices were trying to avoid a decision on such a value-based issue that is at the heart of the relationship between religion and state. The court asked the government to decide on the matter and delayed ruling again and again. Furthermore, even after the court ruled, it accepted the request to hold a further hearing on the issue, both because the interior minister reconsidered and decided to submit a position on the issue and because of its importance.[60]

Kashrut Supervisors

One of the issues that has plagued the kosher food market for many years and that invites criticism of the chief rabbinate's kashrut system is the relationship between the kashrut supervisor and the business he supervises; in other words, who pays the supervisor's salary—the enterprise he inspects or the local religious council that issues kashrut certification? The rabbinate's critics argue that economic relationship between the two parties creates an opening for cheating and corruption. In 2004, the Movement for Fairness in government asked the court to rule that religious councils must pay the supervisor's salary. Thirteen years elapsed before the ruling was issued in May 2017.[61] During these years, the court repeatedly asked and indeed pleaded with the government and the chief rabbinate to decide on their own that the rabbinate and not the businesses supervised would pay the inspectors salary.

When it finally ruled, the court described its long and patient wait to decide:

> The petition has reached Bar Mitzvah age. Thus far, all the efforts to correct what needs correcting have unfortunately and astonishingly proven unsuccessful. An order nisi was already issued in 2008. Moreover, from time to time the solutions raised shrink and the "mountain" of proposals raised in the various decisions, which are not listed as if we were peddlers, has spawned a "mouse" in the form of a pilot experiment today in six (!) businesses; how wonderful! The sad thing is that none of the respondents deny the impropriety of the existing situation, but

---

60 *General Association of Merchants and the Self-Employed* (*supra* note 50).
61 *The Movement for Governance* (*supra* note 51).

"babies have reached the birthstool and there is no strength to bring them forth." (Isa. 37:3).[62]

Here, too, the court made every effort to avoid a decision and issued a ruling only when it was left with no choice.

It is hard to say that the court could not avoid a decision on the grounds that religion and state issues should not be decided in the courtroom.[63] But since the court has been dealing with these issues for decades, such a significant change in its attitude is unlikely. Indeed, critics of the court, especially on the conservative wing, maintain that the court is biased in favor of liberal values and prefers them to Jewish values. These critics continue that if the court wants to deal with religion and state issues, it must do so in a fair or balanced way. Scrutiny of the court's decisions on issues of religion and state does leave the impression that it tends towards liberal concepts. However, that conclusion ignores the broader context of religion and state issues. As has been shown here with regard to all religion and state issues, the institutional regulation of these mattes in Israel has always been by the Orthodox, and today in large part by the ultraorthodox. In this situation, and given the political system's evident inability to reach decisions on these issues, the court has become the refuge of a minority (in terms of its political power and affiliation with the religious establishment) and its last resort.

Religion and the City: The Localization of Religion and State Arrangements

One of the defining features of the de facto (and to some extent de jure) regulation of major religion and state issues is the increase in local control. Significant differences in the regulation and enforcement of Shabbat closures in the public sphere, kashrut services, other religious services, gender segregation in the public sphere, and more marginal issues such as the public sale of hametz on Passover, the closure of places of entertainment on the Ninth of Av, and the sale of pork have emerged as a result of the different characters of cities and communities.

Both before and after independence, many localities had a clear character—religious, secular, socialist, bourgeois, and so on. Sometimes this character was

62 Ibid., 2 of the ruling, quoting the court's decision of March 22, 2017, on the same matter.

63 See Yedidia Stern, "Halachic Access to Policy Issues," *Law and Government* 4 (5756): 215, 230.

shaped by the residents in an ongoing process, but frequently a rural settlement or town was set up out of a desire to create a homogeneous community of a certain nature. The cities, which have always been home to a majority of the Jewish population, are more diverse. In most of them, religious and secular would live side by side, and religion and state relations in the public sphere emerged essentially from historical arrangements, political agreements, and the overall tone of such agreements.

In the past few decades, and even more so in recent years, with the demographic growth of the religious and ultraorthodox sectors,[64] and their increasing tendency to prefer closed communities, the trend towards segregation has accelerated, and more towns and neighborhoods have become clearly secular or religious.[65] Entire new towns with a homogeneous population, most of them for the ultraorthodox, have been established. There are many examples: Tel Aviv, established as a "Hebrew city" marked by a willingness to preserve the Jewish character of the public sphere,[66] has become the "State of Tel Aviv," a city that flies the flag of secularism and whose population is increasingly unwilling to accept the national arrangements on religion and state issues.[67] Givatayim, which used to have a religious population, now has a much more secular character. Bnei Brak, originally a mixed city with a stronger religious affinity, has become overwhelmingly ultraorthodox. In recent years the majority of the population of Givat Shmuel, a small town in the heart of the central region, has been affiliated with the National Religious sector.[68] Mevo Beitar, Beitar Illit, Emanuel, and Elad were established as ultraorthodox towns. Over the last two decades Jerusalem, which once had a mixed Jewish population, has experienced an out-migration

---

64 At the end of 2018, the ultraorthodox population in Israel had reached one million, up from 750,000 in 2009. This is a growth rate of 4.2% per year, compared with a growth rate of 1.4% per year for the general Jewish population; see Gilad Malach and Lee Cahaner, *Yearbook of Ultra-Orthodox Society in Israel* (Jerusalem: Israel Democracy Institute, 2018), 13.

65 See: Larissa Fleischmann and Yuri Govman, "Level of Religiosity by Neighborhood: Residents' Perceptions vs. Reality," Working Paper No. 82, Central Bureau of Statistics, February, 2014; Social Survey 2009, Central Bureau of Statistics, 91. *Bank of Israel Annual Report 2016*, March 2017, 187.

66 Above, p. 40.

67 For example, according to data published by the Tel Aviv Municipality in July 2017, 16% of all students attended religious or ultraorthodox educational institutions, while the national average is about 35% (Tel Aviv Municipality website). See also: Moti Katz, "Why Ultra-Orthodox Leave Tel Aviv," *Ha'aretz*, July 3, 2008; Aryeh Rubin, "Meah Shearim of Tel Aviv," *Kolot*, supplement to *Bakehila*, 13 Nissan, 5769 (Apr. 7, 2009).

68 For example, in the 2019 elections, about 40% of Givat Shmuel residents voted for religious parties (Central Election Commission website: https://votes21.bechirot.gov.il/cityresults?cityID=681). The ratio of religious to nonreligious students in Givat Shmuel is five to one.

of secular residents and natural increase among the religious and ultraorthodox, which has changed its character.[69]

In an ongoing process, this segregation of the religious and secular leads to the erosion of countrywide arrangements and of national regulation of religion and state issues, replaced by regulations suited to the character of each community. On the one hand, secular communities' unwillingness to abide by the existing arrangements pushes in the direction of secularism. On the other hand, the desire of religious communities, especially ultraorthodox ones, to perpetuate their religious character in the public sphere leads to arrangements and practices that did not exist in the past and changes the Status Quo in the conservative direction.

The localization of religion and state arrangements has historical roots. Under the Mandate, when the British authorities did not permit countrywide legislation regarding the Jewish character of the public sphere, such issues had to be handled at the municipal level. After independence, some of these arrangements persisted as part of the Status Quo, but the main responsibility for them shifted from local to national, and guaranteeing the Jewish character of the public sphere became the province of the Knesset and government.[70] Countrywide standards were set for some issues; for others, the possibility of local standards was expanded. Local legislation was insufficient for those who wanted to emphasize the Jewish character of the state, and over the years they endeavored (and failed) to have these issues governed by national legislation. All the same, major issues tend to be determined by a countrywide standard, while allowing some freedom for local regulation.

The aforementioned changes in the geographical distribution of the Israeli population, with entire cities becoming distinctly religious or secular, have led to growing differences between localities in terms of religion and state arrangements. These differences derive from the variation in municipal bylaws and enforcement policies from place to place and effectively create a broad and dynamic range of religion and state relations. Today we should probably speak of "religion and city," rather than "religions and state," relations.

---

69 For example, while 43% of the Jews in Israel define themselves as nonreligious, in Jerusalem only 22% are secular by their self definition. In contrast, while 12% of the Jewish population was ultraorthodox in 2017, the figure for Jerusalem was 35% (see Gilad Malach and Lee Cahaner, *Statistical Annual of the Ultra-Orthodox in Israel 2019* (Jerusalem: Israel Democracy Institute), 12.

70 Ibid., 25.

Local Regulation of the Shabbat

In the chapter on erosion of the arrangements for Shabbat, where I reviewed the development over the years, I also noted with the geographical variation; but my focus was on the national perspective. Here I want to take a different perspective and highlight the localization of these arrangements.

As mentioned,[71] whereas the ban on Jews' working on Shabbat is nationwide, the operation of businesses is regulated at the local level. The "Enabling Law"[72] authorizes municipalities to prohibit economic activity on Shabbat within their jurisdictions. Although the secular population's interest in shopping on Saturdays has been increasing, the bylaws of most local authorities (94%) still prohibit commercial activity.[73] Does this mean that there is no expression of the local character? In fact, this figure is misleading, and the differences in the nature of the Shabbat between localities are dramatic. In some cities, particularly Tel Aviv,[74] economic and commercial activity then flourishes; in others, it is limited. And in some places, mainly ultraorthodox communities, even vehicular traffic is prohibited on the Shabbat and the city is entirely closed. Formal expression of this variation can be found in the different status of cultural and recreational activities in different municipalities. In 83% of Jewish localities, the local bylaws permit the operation of restaurants on Saturday;[75] and 27% allow leisure and recreational venues—cultural activities.[76] In truth, however, municipal legislation provides only a partial picture of the public nature of the Shabbat on the local level. Even where the laws prohibit commercial or cultural activity, mayors often choose not to enforce them.[77] The reality is usually shaped by the local demand for economic activity on Shabbat; there is a clear distinction

---

71 *Supra* 32.

72 This is the common designation of the section of the Municipalities Ordinance that empowers local authorities to permit the operation or require the closure of businesses on the Shabbat on the basis of religious considerations. This authority was reduced somewhat by the amendment to the Municipalities Ordinance known as the "Supermarket Law," enacted due to pressure by the ultraorthodox parties, which restricted the interior minister's power to permit the operation of businesses on Saturdays (Ibid., 34).

73 Gilad Wiener and Shuki Friedman, *Localized Shabbat: Shabbat Laws and the Scope of the Prohibition of Economic Activity in Local Authorities*, Research Report (Jerusalem: The Israel Democracy Institute, November 2018), 21.

74 As mentioned, the municipal bylow allowed for a relatively large amount of commercial activity on Saturdays (above, p. 30).

75 Wiener and Friedman, *Localized Shabbat*, 18.

76 Ibid., 19.

77 Gideon Zeira, Oriana Almasi, Itai Fidelman, Uri Tal-Spiro, and Flora Koch Davidowitz, "Enforcement of the Provisions for the Opening and Closure of Businesses on Days of Rest by Local Authorities," Knesset Research and Information Center, Feb. 6, 2014.

between cities that observe the Shabbat according to halakhah and the many other cities and communities where market forces shape the nature of the Shabbat rest in the public sphere and gave it much more pluralistic nature.

Another difference between cities involves public transportation on the Shabbat. As mentioned above,[78] the Transport Ordinance states that public transportation in Israel will not operate on Shabbat except in non-Jewish areas. The only exceptions to this rule are Haifa and Eilat, where public transportation has been operating on the Shabbat since the establishment of the state. In recent years, in response to the growing demand for public transport and people's unwillingness to accept the current situation, public transport services have been offered in several cities: in some places (notably Jerusalem), by civil society organizations; in other towns (including Tel Aviv, Givatayim, and Herzliya), by the municipality itself.[79]

This situation of their radically different public spheres on the Shabbat has been blessed by the High Court. In its ruling on the amendment of the Tel Aviv Municipal bylaw in order to permit commercial activity on Saturday,[80] Chief Justice Naor and Justice Barak-Erez described the localization of Sabbath arrangements as an appropriate and even desirable process. In their view, the possibility of different arrangements in each city or community is a better way to balance the inherent conflict of interest regarding economic activity on Shabbat. It allows the municipality to create its own "Jewish and democratic" city and to balance religion and other values according to the wishes and needs of its citizens, as city hall perceives them, with each city different from the other.

The localization of Shabbat regulations rest is having immense results. It is no longer possible to talk about the nature of the Shabbat in the State of Israel as a whole—the variation from place to place is too great. Now the discussion is about the nature of the Shabbat in the cities of Israel. The possibility of achieving a better balance of interests and the adaptation of the character of urban space to accord with the residents' preferences are certainly a good thing. But this localization trend has inescapably turned into a "race to the bottom"; in response to demand that will probably always increase,[81] more and more cities will allow

---

78 P. 42.

79 See Moshe Cohen, "Public Transportation on Shabbat," *Maariv*, Nov. 22, 2019.

80 HCJ 6322/14, General Association of Merchants and the Self-Employed v. the Minister of the Interior (published in *Nevo*, Apr. 19, 2017); additional hearing on HCJ 3660/17, General Association of Merchants and the Self-Employed v. the Minister of the Interior (published in *Nevo*, Oct. 26, 2017) (Ibid., 39).

81 A survey by the Guttman Center at the Israel Democracy Institute, conducted in February 2018, found that 61% of Israeli Jews support the opening of private medical clinics on Saturday,

extensive commercial activity on Shabbat, which will change the nature of the Shabbat in the country as a whole.

Gender Segregation in the Public Sphere

In the last two decades, the phenomenon of the exclusion of women in the public sphere has grown. This erodes the Status Quo, which never included or recognized gender segregation. The phenomenon is manifested in various ways: separation of the sexes at events and ceremonies, on public transport, and in medical clinics; separate sidewalks for men and women; exclusion of female singers from performing before a male or mixed audience, because of the halakhic stricture that men may not listen to a woman's voice; and separation between men and women at funerals. Such segregation has always been prevalent among the conservative Orthodox, mainly in towns and neighborhoods that are almost wholly ultraorthodox.

Gender segregation and the exclusion of women in the public sphere has no legal anchor. On the contrary, in most cases such practices are illegal and local authorities act to suppress them. A series of laws and court rulings prohibit discrimination and require equal opportunity for women.[82] The principle of gender equality received concrete and unambiguous expression in a 2014 government decision[83] that adopted the recommendations of a government committee.[84]

Despite the campaign against the exclusion of women, waged through public pressure, legislation, and court rulings, the phenomenon is spreading. In ultraorthodox cities and neighborhoods with an ultraorthodox majority, gender segregation is the norm, and the municipal authorities, who are supposed to represent the state and combat the phenomenon, promote and fund it. Every public event in ultraorthodox towns such as Betar Illit, Modi'in Illit, Emanuel, Bnei Brak, and Elad is gender segregated. In the Beit Shemesh neighborhoods

---

61% support the opening supermarkets on Saturday, and 40% supporting the opening of garages on Saturday.

82 Judgment: Kol Barama, signs in Jerusalem, recent cases—Afula and Haifa in the district.

83 Government Resolution 1526 (March 30, 2014) states the importance of equality for women and the government's grave view of the phenomenon of their exclusion. It affirms that the government is committed to taking steps to prevent the phenomenon and lists a number of measures to do so.

84 "Report of the Ministry Team to Examine the Phenomenon of the Exclusion of Women in the Public Domain," Ministry of Justice, March 2013.

that are overwhelmingly ultraorthodox, there were attempts to enforce separate sidewalks for men and women.

The hallmark of the phenomenon is its local focus. Those who board a public bus in central Tel Aviv and travel to nearby Petah Tikva must pass through the ultraorthodox city of Bnei Brak. During the half-hour journey, they travel between separate planets, from a secular Western city, where the public sphere is open to all, to a conservative ultraorthodox town where the exclusion of women in the public sphere is the norm. This short journey illustrates the effect of the localization of religion and state arrangements and the transformation of common public space into multiple public spaces that are vastly different from one another, depending on the nature of the communities who operate within them. This is another arena in which localization has eroded the Status Quo.

The Rise of Traditionism in Israeli Society

Before and immediately after the establishment of the state, considerable effort was invested in the attempt to write a constitution. A major cause of the failure to do so was the conflict between the religious and the secular with regard to how the document would express the country's Jewish character. The gulf between their positions was vast. On the religious side, Orthodox politicians and rabbis believed that the centuries-old dream of a sovereign Jewish state should be realized through the strong expression of halakhah in its laws and public sphere. On the secular side stood the socialist and centrist parties, ideological secularists who tended to the idea that the place for religious-halakhic Judaism was a museum; they did everything they could to give the young state a secular character.

More than seven decades have elapsed and Israeli society has changed. A 2015 Pew survey, one of the most comprehensive inquiries into religious observance in Israel, found that 40% of Israelis define themselves as secular, 23% as "traditional," 10% as religious, and 8% as ultraorthodox. But those who report that they believe in God and adhere to major religious practices, such as fasting on Yom Kippur, attending a Passover seder, and celebrating other holidays, far exceed the sum of the three nonsecular categories.[85]

---

85 Pew Research Center, "Israel's Religiously Divided Society," May 2016, https://www.pewresearch.org/religion/wp-content/uploads/sites/7/2016/03/Israel-Survey-Full-Report.pdf

In fact, a new model of "traditionism" has emerged in Israel. Traditionism is an identity that derives from sources that surround and become part of a person.[86] Some people are born into it; some choose it. But the choice is immediate and natural. Traditionism is inherently a soft and hybrid identity. It allows for additional identities alongside it and does not require the effort of diligent adherence to norms or practices.[87]

Israeli traditionism meets all these definitions. It is simultaneously religious and secular. It derives from Jewish sources that surround Israelis and that are mediated through Jewish-Israeli channels. It is natural and does not require dichotomous or clear definitions. It neither demands nor obligates adherence to distinct rituals. It allows and does not exclude. In short, it is unique, rare, and very Israeli. By definition, the category encompasses many Israelis: observant persons who tend to view Judaism as a principled but nonbinding code; traditional Jews of Asian and North African descent (Mizrahim), whose practices are already much more in line with tradition; and the secular who find it convenient to adopt a Jewish identity without being bound by a definition that clearly links them to religious Judaism.

The same conclusion is supported by Rosner and Fuchs's recent study,[88] which designates the phenomenon "Israeli Judaism." Their survey found that many Jewish-religious practices have become Israeli practices followed by a significant percentage of Israeli Jews. Some of these practices, such as lighting Hanukkah candles (over 90%), have a more national character. But others, such as believing in God (78%), fasting on Yom Kippur (67%), or maintaining a kosher home (64%), are clearly religious. Rosner and Fuchs conclude that most Israeli Jews are looking for traditions and customs to hold on to; the erosion of ideological and old-fashioned secularism has spawned practices that have much in common with Jewish rituals, but in a more Israeli and less halakhic and less religious format. Whether we call this Israeli traditionism or Israeli Judaism, it clearly reflects a greater awareness of Judaism and the practices and elements of identity it offers Israelis.

---

86 Jacob Yadgar, "The Traditionalists in Israel: Modernity Without Secularism," Shalom Hartman Institute and the Bar-Ilan University Law Faculty, 2010, 13, 19, 48.

87 Shuki Friedman, "Here Is an Update: A Traditional and Democratic State," *Ha'aretz*, Apr. 19, 2018.

88 Rosner and Fuchs called it "Israeli Judaism," meaning the Israeli adaptation of Judaism and the incorporation of Jewish customs into the Israeli identity of most Israelis. See: Shmuel Rosner and Camil Fuchs, *Israeli Judaism: Portrait of a Cultural Revolution* (Jerusalem: Dvir, 2018), 21, 34ff.).

Traditionism is also prominent in the public arena. Most senior Jewish politicians in Israel identify as traditionists and declare that Jewish religious practices are part of their lives,[89] Jewish holidays are important for them, making kiddush and other religious practices are part of their routine, phrases like "with God's help" and "thank God" trip from their lips with a frequency that would not put Orthodox Jews to shame.[90] Whether this is political grandstanding to attract voters or a genuine belief, it clearly has an impact on Israeli life and society.

In popular culture, Judaism and its traditional texts are omnipresent. The playlist of the avowedly secular Galgalatz radio station includes an impressive number of Jewish songs; at the end of every Hebrew calendar year, the roster of top songs and performers always include several songs with religious content and singers who identify themselves as Orthodox or traditional.[91]

Alongside these, in the last two decades, the Jewish Renewal movement, secular "batei midrash" (institutions and programs to study traditional texts) and communities, and Israelis who define themselves as secular have been investing much of their resources and time in creating a new synthesis between their daily secular life and Jewish religious texts. These programs, which operate at the heart of "Israeliness" and on behalf of Israeli men and women, include the Bible, Mishnah, Talmud, and halakhah into their studies.[92]

Taken together, these create a tangible Jewish atmosphere in the Israeli public sphere, which is also reflected in the adoption of a more conscious Jewish identity. This awareness affects the way Israelis view the Jewish identity of the state and their interaction with the religious services it provides. As long as the secular majority were more or less indifferent to its Jewishness, the ceremonies and services provided by the Orthodox chief rabbinate were seen as a necessary evil that could be tolerated as long as their rights were not violated. But with the

---

89 Examples from the recent past: Avi Gabbay, the Labor Party chairman in 2017–2019, says that he is "traditional" (Yishai Cohen, "Avi Gabbay Is Traditional," *Kikar Shabbat*, July 10, 2007, https://www.kikar.co.il/238544.html); Benny Gantz, the chair of the Blue and White list that won more than a quarter of the votes in both 2019 elections campaigns, says that he "makes Kiddush every Friday and goes to synagogue" and "loves the tradition very much" ("Yossi Assoulin 'Makes Kiddush Every Friday,'" *Be-hadrei Haredim*, Feb. 8, 2019, https://www.bhol.co.il/news/974457).

90 Journalist and researcher Avishay Ben-Haim produced a television report on the traditional outlook of the leaders of the Jewish parties in Israel and the use they make of this identity to attract voters (Channel 13, March 13, 2019).

91 See Nissim Leon, "The Social Renewal of Popular Religious Music in Israel," *Israeli Sociology* 16, no. 1 (2014): 155.

92 Naama Azulay and Rachel Werczberger, "Jewish Renewal in the Secular Space in Israel: From a Phenomenon to a New Social Movement," *Politics: An Israeli Journal of Political Science and International Relations* 18 (2008): 141.

growing awareness of Jewish identity came a desire to choose how the Jewish rituals or practices they participate in are celebrated. This led to significant efforts to create alternatives to the religious services provided by the state and the rabbinical monopoly.

The Civil Society Organizations' Challenge to the Monopoly

The deep explanation for the continuing erosion of the Status Quo is that Israeli society has changed, leading to greater secularization of the public sphere.[93] With this background, another factor at work here is the activity of civil society organizations that wish to end the monopoly on religious services by offering alternatives. In the last two decades, various organizations have been advancing religious pluralism in Israel, so that the Jewish citizens of Israel can choose how they wish to practice their Judaism. They include Tzohar, Giyur K'Halacha, and Hashgacha Pratit within the Orthodox community, and Hiddush, Be Free Israel, and Havaya among the non-Orthodox and avowedly secular. All of these are working from the bottom up to alter the provision of religious services, both by influencing people's preferences and by making it possible for them to choose alternatives.

The main areas in which these challenges have borne fruit are marriage, kashrut, and conversion. In all these areas, it is evident that the alternatives created by private organizations have influenced people's choices, but have also induced the chief rabbinate to improve its services. More importantly, the organization's projects have triggered changes in the legal status of the services they offer and their legitimation by the courts or the Knesset.

Marriage

With regard to marriage, as shown above, the rabbinate holds a statutory monopoly.[94] The Zohar organization of Orthodox rabbis was set up to allow couples to marry in strict accordance with halakhah but in a more friendly environment than that provided by the chief rabbinate. The project proved very

---

93 In general, public confidence in the Chief Rabbinate of Israel is very low. In some surveys it ranks as the least trusted government institution. For example, in 2017, the chief rabbinate enjoyed the confidence of only 20% (Tamar Hermann et al., *Israel Democracy Index 2017*, Israel Democracy Institute, 120).

94 Above, p. 50.

successful; over the years tens of thousands of couples have married through it. After a long rearguard battle by the chief rabbinate, the organization received legal authorization to register marriages and its rabbis were recognized by the chief rabbinate as qualified to officiate at weddings.[95]

In 2018, Hashgacha Pratit launched its own weddings project, which goes a step further in challenging the rabbinate's monopoly. It allows couples that wish to marry according to halakhah to do so without registration through the chief rabbinate. Under current law, such a private ceremony without registration through the rabbinate is a criminal offense. Nevertheless, the initiative is in great demand among religious couples who do not wish to have dealings with the chief rabbinate.

There are also non-Orthodox organizations that provide wedding ceremonies and officiants. Some do so according to the rules of the Reform and Conservative movements; others allow the couple to design their own ceremony to suit their religious (or nonreligious) outlook. These options too are gaining popularity.

The challenge to the chief rabbinate monopoly is reflected in the steady decline in the number of marriages through the rabbinate.[96] In 2018, one-third of Jewish weddings in Israel were not conducted through the chief rabbinate.[97]

The rabbinate's monopoly on Jewish marriage and divorce in Israel is still significant. On the formal level, there is no way for Jews to marry in Israel other than through the chief rabbinate. However, the fact that a third of Israeli newlyweds have not done so illustrates the erosion of its status in this field.

Conversion

Recognition of conversion in Israel actually has two aspects: the entry in the population registry, which allows a wide range of options, and the status recorded by the chief rabbinate, which recognizes only conversions through

---

95 The Law to Amend the Marriage and Divorce Ordinance (Registration) (Registration Areas) 2009 (enacted on October 23, 2013) states that a couple can register for marriage in a rabbinical office of their choice; this opened the door for Tzohar to assume this function.

96 According to a report by the Ministry of Religious Services, released on Jan. 8, 2019, there was a 4.7% decrease in the number of couples who registered to marry through the rabbinate in 2017, and a 6.2% decrease in 2018. Some of this can be explained by the decreasing tendency of couples in Israel (as well as throughout the Western world) to marry, but it is clear that much of the decline in registration with the rabbinate is due to the availability of other options.

97 According to data published by New Family. See "About 29,000 Couples Married in 2018 outside the Rabbinate," *Mako*, Feb. 5, 2019, https://www.mako.co.il/women-weddings/Article-3da5ed6a043b861006.htm.

its own religious courts or those its accepts as valid.[98] Although most of the modifications in the Status Quo with regard to recognition of conversions are due to the court, here too civil society organizations have played a major role in challenging the rabbinate's monopoly. Given the plight of the hundreds of thousands of Israelis who are not recognized as Jews by the chief rabbinate and its stringent policy on conversions, those who wish to convert under Orthodox auspices are in a bind. Giyur K'Halachah, established in 2017, endeavors to solve their problem and offers a more lenient path to conversion (and not just for minors, for whom the process is simpler). Its conversions have been recognized by the court, which ordered the state to list those converted by it as Jewish in the population registry.[99] Thus even though the rabbinate's monopoly on Orthodox conversion has not been abolished, it has been cracked, with rival alternatives that effect a change in an individual's legal status and reduce the demand for the chief rabbinate's conversion services.

Kashrut

The case of the rabbinate's monopoly in kashrut provides an excellent illustration of the challenge that civil society organizations pose to the Status Quo and of its erosion as a result of their activities. The chief rabbinate's monopoly on kashrut is enshrined in law.[100] In many cases, it wields its monopoly to impose strict halakhic standards on kosher consumers. In addition to the rabbinate, there are many private kashrut organizations (the various bedatzim) that cooperate with the chief rabbinate and grant certification that supplements the legally mandated certificate from the chief rabbinate. The rabbinate's monopoly is being challenged today by the Hashgacha Pratit organization and its "illegal" certificates. The question of whether they are in fact illegal, as asserted by the chief rabbinate, eventually reached the Supreme Court. It ruled that proprietors can state that their business is kosher; this reduces but does not fully abolish the rabbinate's monopoly.[101] In the wake of the High Court's ruling and Hashgacha Pratit's relative success, Tzohar also began offering kashrut services that compete with the rabbinate. In this realm too, the rabbinate has not totally lost control, but a significant change has certainly occurred: there is more pluralism

---

98 See at length above, p. 65.

99 HF (JM) 65786-03-17, Anonymous v. the Ministry of the Interior et al.

100 See at length above, p. 71.

101 Rehearing by the High Court of Justice, HCJ 5026/16, Gini v. Chief Rabbinate of Israel (published in *Nevo*, September 12, 2017).

in this area than previously and the Status Quo is eroding—again as a result of the action of civil society organizations.

Summary

The stalemate that has kept the Israeli political system from adapting religion and state arrangements to match the current reality has left room for other actors to erode the Status Quo. Given the Knesset's fecklessness on the matter, the Supreme Court has become the only venue that provides remedies on issues of religion and state. Local communities that deem the countrywide arrangements unsuitable for them have found their own solutions; various sectors of Israeli society that have become more aware of their Jewishness are choosing their own Jewish paths; religious pluralism organizations that respond to Israeli Jews' desire to celebrate and experience their religious life in their own way are influencing and changing the situation. All of them are eroding the Status Quo, much of which, even if still enshrined in the law book, has effectively become a dead letter.

6

Religion and State: Is Legislation of Any Use?

Israeli laws that regulate religious norms, whether explicitly or indirectly, are considered to be "religious legislation."[1] As such, they are frequently attacked as assaults on the freedom of religion and denounced as illegitimate by those who see them as religious coercion. As Danny Statman and Gideon Sapir have shown, an analytical-philosophical examination leads to the conclusion that these claims do not rule out the possibility that a state may have valid for promoting religious ideas and norms and even impose them through legislation.[2] Therefore, the brief discussion below is not about the legitimacy of legislation that regulates religion and state relations, but about its ineffectiveness.

As I have shown in previous chapters, the regulation of religion and state relations through legislation began almost immediately after the establishment of the state. I also showed that noncompliance with these laws, or nonenforcement, is rampant.

The most prominent example of the limited effectiveness of laws governing religion and state relations is the spotty enforcement of the Shabbat ban on

---

1 Haim Cohen classifies religious legislation by motive and outcome. For example, the Work Hours and Rest Law serves a religious interest, but the result is social—a weekly day off. See Cohen (Ibid., 14, note 8), 297, 299.

2 See Statman and Sapir (Ibid., 45, note 99), 180.

commerce.[3] Private marriage is another example. As mentioned, the legislation on marriage and divorce was amended in 2013; today, it is a criminal offense to perform a wedding not preceded by registration with the rabbinate. Nonetheless, organizations and individuals continue to conduct such ceremonies and advertise their services. For example, Havaya has conducted hundreds of unregistered ceremonies. In 2018, Hashgacha Pratit followed suit, though its ceremonies comply with halakhah. Although it is clear that these ceremonies violate the law and the evidence of the "crime" is public knowledge, I am not aware of any case in which the law was enforced.[4]

This state of affairs raises two questions. First, why is compliance with these laws and their enforcement so limited? Second, if so, is there any point to legislation about such matters?

The question of the effectiveness of laws in general and the effectiveness of laws as a tool for promoting ideology engages legal scholars, and not only with regard to issues of religion and state.[5] The fundamental question relates to the doctrinal aims of such a law; the corollary question is whether the law achieves them. The answer can be found through an empirical examination of the law's effect on the behavior of those subject to it.[6] In his comprehensive article "The Functions of Law," Joseph Raz suggests that law has four first-order purposes: directing behavior, primarily preventing unwanted behaviors by means of penal and tort law; creating frameworks for communicating details (contracts, property, etc.); providing services and allocating resources (health, education, taxes); and settling disputes that rise when there is no prior agreement between the parties. Raz also refers to the indirect goals of law, such as those that serve the social order.[7] He does not include among the first-order objectives the possibility that the law is intended to influence the design of the public, or the ethical, national, or religious dimension of the state. However, many have seen an indirect influence on ideology as one aim and result of the law, both when

---

3 *Supra* 33.

4 A reality show broadcast in November 2017 ("Wedding at First-sight") put couples through a ceremony that could be considered as meeting the halakhic criteria. Despite the publicity, the authorities did not take any steps.

5 For a file dealing with various aspects of these questions, see Daphna Hacker and Neta Ziv, eds., *Is The Law Important?* (Tel Aviv: Tel Aviv University, 2010).

6 See Hadar Aviram, "Does the Law Achieve Its Goals? Answers to the World of Empirical Research," Daphna Hacker and Neta Ziv, eds., *Is the Law Important?* (Tel Aviv: Tel Aviv University, 2010), 27.

7 Joseph Raz, "The Function of Law," in *The Authority of Law: Essays on Law and Morality* (Oxford: Clarendon Press, 1979), 163.

they are unclear and certainly when they are explicit.[8] So the basic possibility of using legislation in pursuit of ideology is not unfounded.

If we assume that ideological legislation has the potential to influence citizens' behavior, why has this potential not been realized by Israeli legislation that seeks to regulate the public and private space in accordance with halakhah? In other words, why is this legislation of only limited effectiveness?

In an empirical study of the impact of law on human behavior, Yuval Feldman offers three ways in which the law can affect those subject to it: direct influence, indirect effect, and the creation of an internal motivation to comply with it.[9] In the case of legislation governing religion and state relations, the possibility of its effect on what Feldman calls "internal motivation" illustrates the lack of influence of religious legislation, and this may have an effect on compliance with these laws. Although the definition of "internal motivation" is vague, it certainly refers to how the law may generate an internal motivation in its adherents to comply with it. Within this category, one of the most important variables that affects willingness to obey a given law is individuals' group identity and the extent to which they associate themselves with the group that enacted the law.[10] The closer individuals feel to the law-affiliated group, the more likely they are to obey it; and vice versa. But when a law expresses the values of another group, the tendency to obey it decreases. In our case, when citizens do not share the values that the law attempts to promote their internal motivation to obey it decreases.

Neta Barak-Koren also looked at the influence of ideology on the willingness to obey the law.[11] Her empirical study, however, focused on the contrary situation—religious people's willingness to pay the price of disobedience when a law contravenes their religious tenets. It may be inferred from the results of the experiment conducted by Barak-Koren on a case in which the prevailing view is that the origin of the law is a religious order with which the subjects of the law do not identify. In essence, Barak-Koren found that religious people are apt to risk criminal sanctions and violate such laws. This is understandable. They see their religious belief as a prime value for which they are willing to pay a price. But in the case of religious legislation in Israel, flouting the law is driven

---

8 Aviram (*supra* note 6), 51–60. The article reviews the impact of the law as reflected in empirical studies of its ability to drive behavior and influence ideological perceptions, or at least the possibility of their being perceived as legitimate in the public sphere.

9 Yuval Feldman, "Law, Norms and Behavior: On Moderating and Mediating Variables," in Hacker and Ziv (*supra* note 5), 71, 74.

10 Ibid., 107.

11 Neta Barak-Koren, "Does Anti-Discrimination Law Influence Religious Behavior? An Empirical Examination," *Hastings Law Journal* 67, no. 2 (2016): 957, 1010.

not by faith but by a secular ideology that rejects any statutory form of religious coercion.

Studies have shown that the effect of enforcement on compliance has a direct correlation with the intensity of the enforcement. That conclusion may be valid here as well. Without significant enforcement—and, as we have seen, that does not exist—people will have no compunction about breaking "religious laws" and they will be a dead letter.

Alongside enforcement and compliance with these laws, they also bear a price, even in the eyes of their supporters. Enforcement of religious norms by means of civil legislation alienates many people not only from these norms, but also from the values these laws are intended to serve. In other words, religious coercion leads to alienation from Judaism, and Jewish values are not realized through legislation (noncompliance) nor choice (alienation due to coercion).[12]

12 For example, a survey conducted in the summer of 2016 shows that 56% of Jews believe religious legislation distances the public from their Judaism (see Yahel Faraj, "Between Religion and the State," *Davar Rishon*, August 10, 2016).

Conclusion: Separation of Religion and State?

Was there ever a Status Quo of religion and state in Israel? Probably so. But it was short-lived and it underwent frequent changes over time. In practice, for most of the country's existence the Status Quo has served as an imaginary creature for politicians who invoked it in order to avoid the need to discuss religion and state issues.

The major religion and state issues I have reviewed—Shabbat, marriage and divorce, "who is a Jew," conversion, and kashrut—have changed significantly over the years. There has been a decline in the status of the Jewish religion and its visibility in the public sphere, a decline in its religious representation and institutional appearance and the services it offers. As we have seen, the main factors behind these changes have been the High Court of Justice and bottom-up push by civil society organizations and the public. These took place, of course, in the context of dramatic material and value-related changes in the world and in Israeli society, which have had a great impact on these processes.

In most issues, the trend is unequivocal. Its consequences and implications for the relationship between religion and state, however, are less clear. If it continues with such intensity, a de facto separation of religion and state in Israel is inevitable. This trend is reinforced by the stubborn refusal of the chief rabbinate and other state bodies that provide religious services to listen to criticism, and the public distrust in them.

The emerging situation also invites new ideas. The erosion of the Status Quo leaves room for new arrangements in all the areas examined here, and in others. The new arrangements should address both the fundamental question of religion and state relations; namely the location of the boundary between religion and the state and whether state regulation of so many issues associated with religious belief is justified.

Here I would like to propose a different formula than currently exists for regulating the relationship between religion and state.

The central issues regulated by the legislation are: marriage and divorce, conversion, kashrut, burial, ritual baths, rabbinic posts, and various religious services provided by religious councils.[13]

Supporters of these arrangements believe that this is the proper manner to embody the Jewish character of the state.[14] I share this vision, and believe that the Jewishness of the State of Israel can be articulated in statutory arrangements. However, I believe that such involvement should be sparse and aim at attaining a balance between the country's Jewish character and its other values, while considering the cost for religion itself of excessive state intrusion in these areas.[15]

More than seven decades of the operation of religious services in their current form have shown that the mingling of religious and halakhic interests with national bureaucratic mechanisms glorifies neither religion nor the state. Public confidence in the chief rabbinate and the religious services it provides are very low; of all public systems in Israel, it enjoys the lowest level of trust.[16] Many citizens see the system as one that compels them to act contrary to their

---

13 Jewish law regulates other aspects of public life in Israel—notably the Shabbat, the Pork Law, and the Hametz Law—or serves as an inspiration for regulations. On laws that seek to shape the "Jewish character of the state," see Barak Medina and Joel Cheshin, "Religion and State in the State of Israel: A Review of Existing Arrangements," accessed July 21, 2022, https://m.knesset.gov.il/Activity/Constitution/Documents/H24-08-2005_12-09-33_barak1.doc.

14 Statman and Sapir (ibid., 45, note 99) elaborate on the fundamental legitimacy of mixing religion and state.

15 Although Statman and Sapir (ibid.) conclude that religion has a vested interest in being involved in national life, despite the price it pays for this. In my opinion, even if you accept their position, in some cases the price that religion pays for excessive involvement in public life exceeds the religious benefit produced.

16 According to the *Israel Democracy Index 2017*, the Jewish public's confidence in the chief rabbinate was only 20%, making it the least trusted of all state institutions (Herman et al. *supra* note, Hannan Cohen, Ella Heller, Tzipi Lazar-Shawaf and Fadi Omar, *Israeli Democracy Index 2017*, Jerusalem: The Israel Democracy Institute, 2017, 120).
In general, public confidence in the Chief Rabbinate of Israel is very low. In some surveys it ranks as the least trusted government institution. For example, in 2017, the chief rabbinate enjoyed the confidence of only 20% (Tamar Hermann et al., *Israel Democracy Index 2017*).

conscience and even their Jewish faith, which is not that of the Orthodox.[17] Many Israeli Jews dissociate religious services from religion itself. For them, the chief rabbinate, local rabbis, and state religious services are not authentic representatives of Judaism, but bureaucrats and bureaucracies that pursue private or communal political and economic agendas.[18]

I would like to divide the religious services the state provides to its Jewish citizens into three categories: 1) those that have an impact on the Jewish character of the State of Israel and on the future of the Jewish people; 2) instrumental religious services; and 3) the Jewish dimensions of the state's public image. The first category includes conversion and marriage and divorce law; the second category involves other religious services; the third category involves the Shabbat and other less central problems, such as the sale of pork and the closure of business on Tisha be'Av. The difference between the first and second categories is significant: the issues in the first category have potential implications for the integrity of the Jewish people and its future, at least according to the traditional view, which enjoys much support from the Israeli public.

Conversion is the gateway to the Jewish people but also the gateway to the state. The state has a vested interest in controlling the definition of who is Jewish and preventing it conversion becoming a technical means of acquiring Israeli citizenship by virtue of the Law of Return. Hence it is reasonable and proper for the state to be involved in the conversion process and to set parameters for it, despite its religious nature. The same applies to marriage and divorce. Here too there are implications for individuals who receive service from the state, but also for the Jewish community in Israel and its unity.[19] That is, the interest in regulating marriage and divorce is not to ensure that people are not living in sin, but to preserve the integrity of the Jewish community in Israel.[20] As long as

---

17 Statman and Sapir (ibid., 45, note 99), chapter 3.

18 See, for example, Rivka Haze and Orly Benjamin, "'Then I Had to Go to the Rabbinate': Mapping Secular Identities and Gender in Israeli Families in Cohabitation," *Israeli Sociology* 12, no. 2 (2011): 455.

19 Or, as Ben-Gurion wrote in the Status Quo Letter: "All bodies represented by the Jewish Agency Executive will do all that can be done to satisfy the needs of the religiously observant in this matter and to prevent a rift in the Jewish people" (Troen and Lucas, [ibid., 16, note 14])

20 In this context, see also the proposal for establishing a civil union mechanism in a way that respects halakhic principles. See Shahar Lifshitz, *Civil Union*, Policy Study 68 (Jerusalem: The Israel Democracy Institute, 2014). This proposal, which follows the lead of Langenthal's proposal, offers a choice among forms of marriage and can be an appropriate and widely acceptable interim solution.

these issues continue to be regulated by the state, it must be at the national level, but with the possibility of an alternative.

The second category consists of instrumental religious services. These services promote the religious and spiritual wellbeing of individuals who need them. In my opinion, whether such services are provided by state or by private bodies will not affect Israel's identity as a Jewish state: it will be a Jewish state even if the kosher market is privatized or ritual baths fall under the jurisdiction of the Ministry of Health.

Kashrut for the general public, too, falls into this category.[21] It is not the state's affair whether or not a person wants to eat kosher food. Whether food is kosher concerns those who eat it, and no one else. More stringent standards, less stringent standards, or kashrut provided by a trusted body—none of that can affect the character of Israel as a Jewish state.

Therefore, the state should not be involved in defining standards for products that require certification for those who observe kashrut, nor the appropriate stringency. Furthermore, as mentioned in chapter 1, the state's involvement in the halakhic question of kashrut regulation detracts from halakhah and infringes on the religious freedom of rabbis, for example when the court imposes a specific kashrut standard on them. What should engage the state in this regard is consumer protection and the services it provides to citizens. Since many Israelis eat kosher food, the state needs to ensure that everyone can find food complying with their standard and trust the certification.[22]

With regard to the third category, the public image of the State of Israel, two main interests can be identified. The first is injury to the religious sensibilities of Shabbat observers, for example when motor vehicles traverse religious neighborhoods on Shabbat; the second is the state's public image. The first is a matter of citizen's rights;[23] the second, the realization of a religious-social vision of sectors of the Jewish public while taking account of the rights of other sectors (for example, the violation of freedom of movement in the absence of public transport). Obviously, if new arrangements are not found, there will be a downward spiral and the Jewish expression of the Israeli public image will be eroded. Here too, however, the balance of values must be taken into account: both the variation among localities and the social values that are impacted alongside the erosion of the Shabbat. Despite the religious origins of the

---

21 Unlike kashrut in public institutions and official settings, on which I will elaborate below.

22 For a detailed proposal for regulation in this vein, see Finkelstein and Friedman (ibid., 72, note 208), 116.

23 *Horev* (ibid., 45, note 98).

Shabbat, its negation signifies the loss of a valuable cultural and social asset that most Jews in Israel would like to hold on to.

After more than seventy-four years, the time has come to regulate religion and state relations in Israel. The Status Quo has been eroded so severely that it can no longer provide a solution or even mask the issues, both old and new; new agreements must be reached. These agreements should express a broad common denominator among the Jewish majority, while taking the non-Jewish minority into account. It is also quite clear that they cannot be reached by means of coercion and the political power of minority groups, religious or secular, on the extremes. Only a broad coalition of leading politicians and the Israeli public itself can institute such agreements and redeem Israeli society from the fierce struggle that has plagued it since the establishment of the state.

Index

CPSIA information can be obtained
at www.ICGtesting.com
Printed in the USA
LVHW082142220223
739975LV00001B/2

9 798887 190891